MW00608767

CONTINENTAL SHELF

SHORTER POEMS
1968-2020

•

HENRY GOULD

DOS MADRES

2022

DOS MADRES PRESS INC.

P.O. Box 294, Loveland, Ohio 45140
www.dosmadres.com   editor@dosmadres.com

Dos Madres is dedicated to the belief that the small press is essential
to the vitality of contemporary literature as a carrier of the new voice,
as well as the older, sometimes forgotten voices of the past. And in an
ever more virtual world, to the creation of fine books pleasing to the
eye and hand.

Dos Madres is named in honor of Vera Murphy and Libbie Hughes,
the "Dos Madres" whose contributions have made this press possible.

Dos Madres Press, Inc. is an Ohio Not For Profit Corporation and a
501 (c) (3) qualified public charity. Contributions are tax deductible.

Executive Editor: Robert J. Murphy

Illustration & Book Design: Elizabeth H. Murphy
www.illusionstudios.net

Typeset in Baskerville & Helvetica Neue
ISBN 978-1-953252-66-1
Library of Congress Control Number: 2022943520

First Edition

Copyright 2022 Henry Gould
All rights reserved. No part of this book may be reproduced or transmitted in
any form or by any means graphic, electronic or mechanical, including photo-
copying, recording, taping or by any information storage or retrieval system,
without the permission in writing from the publisher.
Published by Dos Madres Press, Inc.

ACKNOWLEDGEMENTS

The author gratefully acknowledges prior publication of these poems in the following journals :

Pastoral; Acc # 14; Going South on US 61 : Talisman (Blake School). *For March 19th; The Priests; Beep Beep the Baby's Up; Trumpets; If You Could See That Porch; A Successful Egg Hunt; Aimless; Summer; "the well is always there"* : Hellcoal Press (chapbook). *when music breaks; Old Song; X; Night Garden; Self-Portrait; Finished; Poem; Hue; Memorial Day; Lousanna; Prehistoric* : Copper Beech Press (*Stone* : book). *Epistle; The Riddle* : Northeast Journal. *For the Ones who Dig* : Situation. *Ocean State* : Newport Review. *Ocean State; Water Mirror; Joseph Brodsky; Stars in the Earth* : Providence Journal-Bulletin (newspaper). *Hieroglyph* : Clerestory. *Triptych for Elena Shvarts* : Alea. *All Clear* : Fulcrum. *Atlantis; Everything, Everywhere* : Ofi Press Magazine (Mexico City). *Jozef Czapski; Autumn* : DiVersos (Aguas Santas, Portugal). *Waire; Under the Sun; Notes; Late Summer; Ballade Industriel; Everything, Everywhere* : Tourniquet Review.

to Sarah Keisling

TABLE OF CONTENTS

I

BABY STEPS

(1960s)

old . men sit on . rocking chairs breathing through
leaf-burn-smoking pipes . sifting Western skies
through ash.an amputated hill groans.behind the .
rusty-nailed shack . half green, half dug . dirt .
a dog barks   a lean jaded horse.
in . his sleep   PASTORAL   jaggles giggling
at a black   from a black .
train, bambling down . the track chug-chogging .
loud . a jeans (faded) . boy watches . rubs dirt
on . his face.

—

ACC. NO. 14 FOR 3/21/69

a tall creosoted tree
tangent to an irregular steelglass
object which is bent
out of shape
gray concrete rolls out following
redgreenblue objects of flat steel
black shiny object with red flashing
dome
on top   two blue objects   congruent
with boots   they move around
communicate
other similar figures   many of them
move around also   they communicate
dumb bastards   can't they read
the roadsigns?

GOING SOUTH ON U.S. 61

rusted rails running to
Moose Lake, Bruno, Willow Creek
North Branch, Stacy, Forest Lake.
white farmhouse wanders among
clusters of contraptions –
a dirty once blue pick-up sits
on concrete blocks
a crazy useless tractor, one wheel
sunk in spring mud
a wind vane creaks on a pole.
the brown once red barn
slides sloping into earth again.
restless freeway roars between
Moose Lake, Bruno, Willow Creek
North Branch, Stacy, Forest Lake.
where screaming metal screams past
screaming glass, and billboards flash
sun-scorched, unread scrawls.
dairy queens stretch their spray-paint
crowns across the road, one last try
before they die in the darkness behind.
telephone poles crash bravely through
the barrier, and men in blue shirts dig holes.
the stop lights are always green
and the towns
Moose Lake, Bruno, Willow Creek
North Branch, Stacy, Forest Lake
speed by without breathing.
brown brick
Joe's Bar-B-Q

gray grain elevator
then gone, flashing dull.
when they have gone,
only the gray, billboarded, roadsigned
tongue remains –
always running, running to another
Moose Lake, Bruno, Willow Creek
North Branch, Stacy, Forest Lake.

WAIRE

I appeared once to myself
as a wracking thirst and
spent the day devising ways
means of forcing
and pressing that green
depth, depthless square
of green into my waiting black head.
It's all in the depth,
you know he said
the mirage silver mirror
line between the
green depth, green &
aching open joy of blue.

HIGHSCHOOLSCRAWL

I've often idly gazed
at loud red-painted boxes
or silver handles or superb chairs
while green ivy silently wanders
through my foolish hair.

Oh crimes. I'll dash my foot
through the aluminum hedge,
you'll screech like an old train.
Oh deeth. My tooth which once
told me tales now wears earrings.
Oh miners, you carry your caves
inside you, your eyes turned to lanterns.
Oh hear, the sound hides
behind the sight, the groan
behind the eyes, between the eyes.
Oh madness. You turn like a leaf.

BLAKE SCHOOL CHAPEL SPEECH

Hi there glad you could all come
just straighten your ties and listen to a tale
my name is Prester John
I'm a king from deepest africa
ancient coptic christian
in heathen jungle,
where tigers and tarzan
compete for prize money,
while cameras roll and monkeys scream
I'm Prester John
son of the magi
magi that's right magic
teller of lies/teller of truth/teller of lies
so just straighten your ties and listen

I'm an old man
once I was young rolling in hay
heaving bright air through fields
bones of beasts not yet risen burned
me through laughter, silence.

…
then one day
then one day the day turned aquick black
then back again new before I knew
I was pounding in the dark and afraid
but I could not go back to Smileand.

I pounded and frowned and groaned
pounded and groaned and frowned
groaned and frowned and pounded.
I moved slowly into enclosures of steel
then quickly broke them down
fearing dreams and fearing days
writing my name in different ways

...

then one day
then one day I awoke to the dream
of the ancient earth Quakers
I cracked like a fissure,
hooked on my own worm like Jonah
in my own new whale.

(my name remember is Prester John, priest john.
your neckties are asleep. wake up and listen.)

so I climbed fresh-blaked on a bright bus
which wound its way toward Washington
where we meant to carry candles, chant
and further exorcise the place.
we shall be a million strong, we sang
and we shall overcome. we rode like children.

...

and then
and then far back deep under the dark
rear of our bus arose a flower
arose a dark, dark lady on a seashell
from beneath the green seat

a dark, dark lady riding a seashell
a dark, dark lady riding a shell
and she drew me and drew me and drew me
back, back into the bus, back, back, back
back, back into the bus, back, back, back, back, back

(Wake up! Remember! I am Prester John,
mythical ruler in northern rockies
a holy flower colony of children
where our own few seeds sprout, and
we survive and live and grow.)

So she drowned me
and my lady and I were lost
and I was lost, and white Washington
temples were lost and we awoke
exhausted in Ithaca, New York.
I read the news of Washington,
groaning in Ithaca nowhere.
My dark lady laughed her rage
and screamed her laughter
into frozen nights.
So I went away, away, away, away.

Wake up! This is the last time! Remember!
I'm an old man making food
in my children's colony, bearded
like Moses or Ulysses or Prester John
I rule my flower children with a fist
so they may survive in wilderness.
but my days grow yellow.
my children are not sane.

the ground lies fallow, while
my sons steal down the mountain to find
a hamburger stand, and my eldest now,
he wears a coat and tie, and my youngest, now,
he wants to be a business man, and my daughters, now,
they want to go to school…

December 1969

when music breaks
through stiff halls
crumbling flags under
the wild bright sea

flowers burst
through cold stone

and time is wrapped
in warm summer

II

EARLY POEMS
(1970s)

FOR MARCH 28 NINETEEN 71

after reading Apollinaire

I made this notebook thoughtlessly
out of marks that separate me
from what my feet touch
though it bakes my eyes
each morning leaving a room
I find a lot of people without shoes
are whistling down the street
without caring about stars or dark bowls
a girl's hair beckons the evening on

in the warm air the first fly of spring
drones about my face looking for summer
short-legged people with winter hats
glance at the sun and bounce off the sidewalk
my back to a warm wall
I know how silence defeats love
leaning like an old man
against a warm day like this

BEEP BEEP THE BABY'S UP

you can do anything you want.

the baby here is trying to decide

about growing up human. he's rubbing

his double chin, he's a serious kid.

in a house on Arthur St.

a cap pistol is sitting on a desk

in the bedroom upstairs with the yellow

walls. according to the kid here

it's supposedly waiting

for the little green men.

the sky gets closer

as it gets more blue,

and you can recall

the 4th of July

all the heat

and all those little flags

THE PRIESTS

We found a narrow path for each year to travel on,
the days sloping into each other, a horse steps down a hill.
Each new year trembling like a wet bird, in colors
dazzling and negative, of people and wide streets.

We built resting places for old cripples with sacks.
Disgust or joy slides like surf across the faces of the poor.
Temples were piled up with small, touching objects
which we gave to girls on the street.
More and higher stone delights rise into the sky,
which rains. Sampans and ketches bobbing in the blue harbor.

In the country, vague tremors in the well-yard, odd clouds.
Finally, just as he predicted, as he sighed his last
out through the hut door: white ships glide into the bay.
Stars bump quietly. Wooden docks, the boulders on the shore.

TRUMPETS

trumpets   above clouds
above the trees below   the dash
a bicycle is yours   the race won
miles from the starting-point
the Romans   drums in the statues
that face   grimacing in peace

terrible horns

"why did it now…"   boulevard
of heat   "who I knew" once
a letter   signed in, in somewhere
in the South   stood there
as   "by the way"
born in Iowa
this tree   in the hall
above, wouldn't these horns
"be quiet"

IF YOU COULD SEE THAT PORCH

to MRG

If there is something blue
between a cloud and a painting
the full sense of a silent moment
appears suddenly like rain.
It goes over the land
it sings a tune you learned too
standing on the wet porch.
Little clowns in yellow raincoats
the laugh of a hidden yard
a girl in blue goes by
the big world raining
beyond the porch
in those yellow raincoats,
the things you always forget
because morning is full of birds.

A SUCCESSFUL EGG HUNT

keep reminding me
that the weather needs no weathermen
and cats have no masters: they
don't need wisdom either.
tell me again:
the inside of a plum is warm-blooded
and constantly melting.

I have received your messages of love –
as they leave your lips
they dissolve my skies.

AIMLESS

the obvious chord
to your last year on earth
will be glad.
the extensions you built
as the sun came up
will prove empty,
but golden.
the butterflies are aimless
this summer, but each one
reaches Mexico in the fall.
who taught you to speak?
who asks you. as if
the air is yours,
the corn has ears.
at the beach one day
the puzzle of the bathers
fits into the afternoon:
in their tight wet suits
they watch the sun on the silver lake,
                      bubbling up

SUMMER

The child lies in the green yards
as clouds fill the sky,
make it round, looming down,
shying away, or drifting off.

There are no mountains.
On the porch a sleeping cat
rolls over, into the sunlight.
Flies buzz. Around noon
he looks in a window,

a piano leans against a wall
of the blue-green room.

OLD SONG

"I want to stay –"
he cries, the willows
rattle and play and the voice
is carried far away downstream.

Downstream, in autumn,
the bums are coughing, and smoke
for the wisps that rise
and cool; they stay awhile.

They lie and cough,
the willows play, the sun
is red – rattle rattle
go away, go away.

The story is for winter
to forget, when woods are dark
and snow is lightest in the darkness
– and that light is deep.

X

The trees along the street
on the rising ground,
in the last light
darkening the houses –
a miniature world,
a tiny sphere
somewhere.

I see the little people,
child people, small people –
and the crossroads.

NIGHT GARDEN

The clear night sky shines
so bright, a distant surface
is revealed, a silver arch
where a mind meets the sight.

And I become a creature,
a walking long-nosed poor liar,
something entering other things
like breath in the heart chambers.

Animals and the foliage fall
to whispering in the little light;
no motion below disturbing,
the slow heavens revolve.

SELF-PORTRAIT

I reject the close close-up,
drawing back from the map
of mundane decay – bad skin.
For a moment the lips favor
kisses stolen from heaven –
but on reflection, killing time,
they break into the grinning
man of little faith. Buckteeth
seal my bond. I am one
with the hell of animals,
weird rhinos, giraffes, gazelles
trapped in the oven, the bloody
reservations in the final drought.
As I turn away, hunched-over Man,
98-pound Mr. Atlas, globe head,
overcoat, no bones – a shadow
of a fleeting glimpse, there
where once you paused, holding
your charm in my arms for me –
the eyes, the last illumination
before this image fades, boy
drowns in a pool, in the myth.

FINISHED

The scarecrow shivers
in the summer heat, nailed up,
stretched out on wooden poles,
a bundle of smoking straw.

Below him thrives a tiny city,
green vaulting walls and waving
spires, quick bees transporting
vital news in the precious dust.

In the cool darkness of trees,
quiet gods attend to the harvest,
and for them, brilliant flowers
swing like plumage on his wings.

But for him, it is finished:
all that remains is to raise
a stern brow at madcap birds,
and cast a slowly-turning shadow.

POEM

Why are the plains like memory,
and the sea like a daydream
where the sun breaks in pieces
of old musicals, blind summers?

The farmhouse far from the ocean
carries my death on waves of wheat,
and bears a heavy childhood too,
bearing a heavy child, my fields –
where we look away to
when the tools are put down
and our hands are free.

When the head leans on the doorpost
and the arms are folded, almost waiting,
the mind could become a river flowing south
and shaking with that human sound.

HUE

Words kind as rain pour down
from mothers and fathers of gentle eye.

Bees have hidden in the hive's head
a little sunlight fallen on the field.

Small planets hover in the immense
blue Pacific of starlit… ; morning

mumbles rustling branches of night
into morning glories, and a rose

resides, lightly bearded with snow,
on the ancient wall above your door.

MEMORIAL DAY

Statue standing grey in summer rain,
wrinkled stone worn by many seasons,
brow, shoulders, backbone full of purpose,
memory shivering in the roar of battle,
emblem of endurance everlasting,
lasting now in peacetime summer rain.

Rising in the shadow of the trees,
mist of thoughts returning from the dead,
comes to life within the broken heart,
comes to join the living and the dead,
statue of the mystery of glory,
statue standing grey in summer rain.

LOUSANNA

Indignant policemen arrest
a stalled Mardi Gras –
spring rolls in, a carnival
in a private shadow
of the vast land of sleep.

Tuesday is fat. This
is a display of weakness –
certain necks turn red.
Honorable generals
arrange a state funeral.

Lent comes too fast.
The democratic party's over.
Texas bouncers, cold
as metal, rusted Romans,
prepare the sacrifice –

let us honor the thin blade,
the man-made clock,
the traditional feast,
the secret society, and
the undertaker's guild.

Then this masquerade
for an illusory season,
martial feast, flimsy
holiday on ice, is lost
in chords of Easter guitars.

PREHISTORIC

They lived on the sea.
Dolphins understood the liquid
flight, earth-shaped in the hands
of the aquamarine. Whispers
and cast-up shells, echoes
and pearls of turning stars.
Rising and floating suspended
like a bridge on steel threads.

This was before and during
the flood, and remained after
in the memory of rivers –
historical driftwood
and the forest of trees,
Armadas of pines, fleets
of Turkish galleons, meeting
Mediterranean on the ocean floor.

...the letters add to the elegance of a structure,
even if their meaning is hid from those not
familiar with the language. Here, they tell
how a piece of the true Cross was obtained at
Constantinople in 1034 and enshrined in the
Chapel, where each night prayers were to be
said until Christ came again. About half of
the Chapel has collapsed, the interior yawning
hollowly in the direction of the Soviet Union.
— Horizon Magazine, *Winter 1971*

the well is always there
a decade of water
just a well
the soldiers pass by
and today the girls are among the clowns
each hiding an arm or wearing a red dance
standing around the well always there

III

REAGAN YEARS

(1980s)

WINTERTIME

Wintertime.
Snow fell silently down.
The town was covered, the roads,
the hills, the steeple, the graveyard.
The cars were dead,
and people went about in simple cloaks.

A coin was minted from scrap,
a large metal coin for honest work.
No one produced – the earth gave,
there were heavenly gifts.
Wisdom and knowledge appeared
in the shade of the vine.

Violin, harp and drum
carried a quiet sound
over the rooftops, into the forest.
It was a bitter cold winter.
Snow fell silently down.
The town was covered, the roads,
the hills, the steeple, the graveyard.

SEASONAL

Late summer looming,
the curling foam of slow clouds on the horizon.

The decline of gentle things,
the hidden fall of a sparrow in low thickets;
the willow's drooping head, lost
in reflections stolen by the stream;
the blue shadow of northern pines,
offering thorny palms to a far-off, iron sky.

In the sound of hesitant rain,
bearing sad news which cannot be withheld,
broadcast over the dry fields by broken seed-pods,
I hear my own small steps;
I fall in the spiral flame of leaves,
red blaze to match the sun, bury the flower-stalks,
and mark the bees' grave in the sleeping mound.

Then, when the stars have swung their turn,
I will rise with the breaking of the early ice,
brushing off snow, bright bitter blues, and winter sun.

AMERICAN SCENE

The sky is gray the wind is blowing
The cars in the yard are hunkered down

A little girl is gathering leaves
At the edge of a bent field near her home

The big lone oak is almost bare
Its craggy branches toss and brood

The little girl walks against the wind
Over the trailer park low clouds roll by

It's quiet out here in the country

LIFE IN THE MIDWEST

This is my house,
and there's only one door.

One door for morning,
the very early morning – you remember.

One door for evening,
the deep sad evening – you remember.

A house is only a house.
A door is only a door.

BOSCH

after Rimbaud

The sunset of the Empire.
Evening of extinction for strange,
outmoded animals. Green pyramid
resting, lightly sleeping on the currency.

Workers are constructing machines
for smooth transportation over landscapes
and placement among trees and fountains,
Florida lagoons of decrepit years.

The landed gentry celebrate with cymbals and swords
the crepuscular myth of mountainous pride.
Engineers instruct their apprentices
to leave no traces of magic to posterity.

Engines of seething anger!
A broken eggshell gaping like a cave,
belching black fumes ignored by the prince
and princess in their fond retirement.

The elders of the land cannot transmit
a forestry of sensibility which is no more,
and the sunset of the Empire will take place
within the body of this anguished beast.

EPISTLE

You,
tender friend,
a small body
traveling
over and under
the dense mythologies
of sad children.

You,
a child yourself,
a balancing
flamingo, one foot
in the pool of wisdom
out of the kisses
of babes and bees.

Don't let the crime
fit the punishment –
you don't deserve
the grieving oil,
and the shackles
and the chains
will rust to dust.

In the forest
of reality coming,
you will find
a bright key
lost in the grass –
the dense mythologies
of sad children.

LITTLE SUN

for Alexander

Only just arrived from the milky way
and still dwelling in the mountains,
the soft hills of the small planet
of your mother – you can relax,
your cradle snug in the branches;
all around you vague motions,
sounds of mingling birds or people;
over your head a bright mobile, swaying
and glittering like a sailing ship.

Only just lifted from the river,
still rocking with the evening ripples,
at that quiet hour when the earth
settles down to dream – who are you?
An echo of some voice, a reflection
at the water's edge, in Egypt,
in the wilderness, in the milky way –
your little boat bumping the shoreline,
floating to the ocean sound asleep.

Only just delivered from your absence,
lifted from the mineshaft, from empty space;
only now beginning to awaken, to remember
all these familiar rhythms; just lifted
from the water and now lifted and held
aloft in your father's arms – still
almost weightless, but gaining momentum,
little planet, little sun, coming down
to bear the full weight of the earth.

THE RIDDLE

for Phoebe

It has happened so far in the future
our clocks cannot find it,
despite their slow and steady pilgrimage.

It is recognizable only in dreams,
and achieved only after angelic flight
(which comes almost to the same thing).

It happened so long ago, in secret —
our emergence from the salt,
our glimpse of black fields and curving seas.

When we become like angels,
borne slowly along like fish in the poet's dream,
we will recover that buried surprise.

It is the past waiting to be delivered,
the future's murmuring descent —
and a ring which rises from these two deeps.

OUT OF ORBIT

The old man without a home is shouting
through the plate glass of the new restaurant,
waving his arms, condemning them all
for obscure crimes of which they are innocent.

The new manager, his hair neatly combed
and his soft face like a washed mushroom,
gets confused and starts waving his arms too,
furiously apologizing to his customers.

Finally, the old man staggers away.
Up in the dark sky, the stars are falling.

ILL AUGURS

(circa 1982)

A president steps out carefully
from behind a palm tree in Hollywood

Reciting his lines in his sleep
Crossing the Delaware, crossing the Styx

Overhead in the gym George Washington
Looks on transfixed in heaven unable to move

While a voice oozing with milk and syrup
Embalms the children with unctuous praise

They are cheering their first mandate
And he poles along, the boat seems to cross

Drink from the waters of Lethe he tells them
Forget your country's dying into life

Outside the oranges are freezing in Florida
Even the obvious weather is upside down

The great white capital is iced over behold
Earth turning a cold shoulder on our feasts

FOLK SONG

We were dreaming, and
the day was long and empty –
like a wise field, like a big ballpark
in a little town, hiding in the midwest,
drifting through a night carnival of stars.

Or maybe only I was dreaming,
and you were only waiting for a train –
walking on the platform, humming
one of those songs about rivers,
one of those old tunes about trains.

But I was sure I was awake that night,
under the stars and their lonely music –
in that cold little town on the frosty plains,
standing at the station, leaning out
listening down the long straight tracks.

UNDER THE SUN

The megaphones of the demagogues
create a new space over the grasslands,
a flat waste of abrupt authority,
a one-way highway into boxes of the mind.

There, with an iron adhesion,
the lockjaw of an angry will
and magnetized puffery of prestige
unite with a bit of crisis management

to form a glutinous ministration
of upright pipe-dreams, pep rallies
entering the maelstrom, pagan science
magnifying the divine body,

a visage of the ordinary emperor,
vacationing in lonely places
where the earth settles down to sleep
under the foot-stomps of the believers.

GAMES OF THE SUN

All afternoon
small clouds of dust
descended, settling on
the road. We watched the sun
play games with them, yellow
beams guiding them down
to join the rubble. And we
never wanted to run away.
We blazed – tiny motes
of happiness. Summer
spoke in our reedy voices,
feverish, delirious,
while dragonflies hammered
at the gates of the sky.

NOTES

If I begin to speak to you
without blurring the sounds,
without shouting out lies.

The hill is the road's father.
The valley was my mother's path.

The stars do not smudge the night,
they wheel slowly on their lost trails.
They are silent tonight, grace notes
of a deeper composition. Listen –
now they begin to tune the instruments.

The road was my father's hill.
The path was my mother's valley.

PRAYER

As I go out walking
from morning to night
let me sing of your splendor
with all my might

LATE SUMMER

Evening makes way for night,
and outside, the wind
is bringing autumn in from Canada,
the last of the ice-cream trucks
rattles home to Johnston,
ringing its off-key chimes.

The locusts are all gone.
The crickets are still turning
spirals in the inner ear.
Children still go to bed thinking
about the first day of school.

And the world fills with helium,
heading out on its long journey
over the hills, into the cool
sky – weightless now, letting go
the ballast – an enormous yesterday.

VOLUNTEERS

You disappeared into the neighborhoods
Impelled by a clean simple thought
As quiet as fog coming over the harbors

It was something you had in mind
And it pleased you with a pure anonymity
Something belonging to everyone by right

Or it was a music you heard at home
Traveling over the treetops and the walls
Rising out of the busy heart of the past

The quaint fiddles of the immigrants
And all those echoes of the Appalachians
Soaring over the heaviness in labor

All the dull and fearful experiences
Somehow transfigured in that childish way
Of light dance steps and good humor

And a pride you had in presenting this
Among other talents at the Talent Show
Drawing out praise like the Beloved One

As quiet as fog coming over the harbors
Impelled by a clean simple thought
You disappeared into the neighborhoods

MIRROR

Look at the intricate carving
in the rich dark wood –
must go back to the 18th century,
at least!

But the surface appears
to be a recent invention –
smoother than water,
finer than glass.

You have to stand still,
try to collect yourself…
can you hear me whispering
from the other side?

IV

WAY STATIONS

OCEAN STATE

Here the waters gather along the shore.
They meet the land breathing in foam,
and roll the sleepy pebbles and shells
back into long sand waves as before.

Our moon, casting her antique spells.
A motionless iris in the whale's eye
of the sea, her unspeakable name
sinks to the bottom of lonely wells.

Her low whispers frame the deserted dome.
Her light covers the circus floor.
And she lifts, with one nocturnal sigh,
the heaving swells in a silver comb.

                    *

It is moonlight in the darkness,
and the heart finding after midnight;
it is a boat unmoored on the water,
and the current circling by itself.

It is tomorrow; it is a light word
floating through an open door,
and the wind moving in the quiet,
whispering over the land of the dead.

                    *

Bees dance above closed lips;
in the clear shadow of the oak
wherever they turn their heads
they follow the bright pattern.

Quietly, by the granite cistern
under a crowded canopy of reds,
in the cool wind a broken spoke
sways whichever way it slips.

*

To give back to the rain
what was announced on the rooftops
in whispers, at the end of May–
the rain, a drowsy origin
cradled in the huge bronze
and silver of twisted beech.

Your sounding, not like laughter
on dry streets, nor an obituary
reminiscence, give and take
of battering wind–but slight
drumming on rough graves, midway
from the obscure haze of a lamp.

*

A slow wind blows through the night,
carrying summer in puffs of sighs.
Far off there in the valley hollows
a yellow lamp swings to and fro.

Tree-bark, tree-limbs creaking,
the muffled sounds in the warm air,
and overhead thin clouds hurrying
under a wheeling shroud of stars.

Day will impress our crafty cities
with silver and bronze, the filigree
of spiderwebs, moldering iron,
the legible engraving of farewells.

Night, and heavy-hearted woodlands,
and the rustling of uncut grasses
in the children's books, a lamp
throwing a wide circle in the wind.

*

Halloween. The sun's already down.
Everywhere leaves are gathering,
lightly rustling and shivering,
their ruddy bloom already fading,
the sun's dry wine drunk to the dregs.

The neighborhood grows anonymous.
Soon the small ghosts will appear,
flickering and half–transparent
under the streetlights, costumed
for space travel, or the Middle Ages.

This is that ancient harvest night.
Harvest of time, harvest of souls.
Tonight the years are buried quietly
under a shroud of old leaves, and I
am a child too, standing at the door.

*

Time now for the trees to shroud the earth
with their dark branches, time
when the wind dies down,
and over the still mirror
a faded voice is whispering.

Time again to climb into the old
music-box in the forest,
and wind the iron spring—

it is letter by letter,
line by line.

*

The wind for France
blusters and laughs.
Green hills, gathered
and chaste, gleam
over the humped sediment.

And bowmen will carry the day.
Silence an awkward gesture
among the clear circles,
at the lighted feast
of modesty and honor.

Only, in the mild air,
to say goodbye. Or there,
in grandmother's book,
Rapunzel, glancing down
from her strange tower.

Or stars over the sea.
Or tongues of fire.
A hearth-blaze. Fold
my hands, light the
four corners of the bed.

*

The poet is monotonous, his head
resting on her empty sleeve,
his voice out of the mineshaft
muttering rumors of precious gems.

And stars shine in the black sky,
peacefully, released at last
from that deep unspoken gloom
by his aimless, undying lament.

*

EPITAPH

He set his hand to many
treacherous decrees,
and made many enemies
among nobles of good family.

Quarrels being the cement
of state, after the blood-
scrawl of a name is understood:
honorable Gloucester, noble Kent.

Yet who will rise to condemn
this prince of liberty's decay?
With a mortal wound he lay
by the seashore, crying "Jerusalem!

*

at noon

Orpheus sings alone,
his lyre left in the wind
moaning in elliptical harmony.

Persephone sleeps, her head
hidden in her arms, and shadows
of clouds passing over her hair.

And John, in his prison, hears
dance music in the rooms above,
and the sound of an axe on stone.

*

They are nobody's children,
and they walk with your airplanes,
they touch your shadows.

Nobody heeds them,
they were born on the west side
of the train, in a heavy rain.

They are your time.
Their eyes close on your flag.
They will take no names.

They are nobody's children.
God is the worm in their hearts,
they were born of the Virgin.

*

from a cave

Such a small voice,
I would not stop to hear;
the sun was going down, and
there were no houses near.

Such a strange voice,
whispering out of the ground–
familiar, though it seemed
unearthly, utterly profound.

Such a sweet voice,
twining my cavern ear;
a vine for water jars, when
all the wedding guests are here.

*

Summer was ocean, a deep gift,
incubation of Joshua, solstitial parakeet.
And earth was borne into heaven,
vaulted into heaven on boats of reeds.

And this May light in the neighborhoods,
where a flowering clematis mantles the porch
in curls of shade, is preparation –
enjoins old bones to climb the coruscating tree.

*

The child honoring you in dreams,
embrasure of innocence, tender shoots
of early radiance – your figure
landscape, unfamiliar town, scent
of May lilacs along a worn road.

Not to be known yet,
only a heavy cloud pregnant
with summer rain
(iron mortality, rust
of decline not yet to be);

gathering up your skirts
you make your way, slow path
beyond the jealous decorations,
fever of scorn, offended pride,
dry branches crackling – a bonfire.

*

The wind exhaled, this world
sprawled – a spring disaster, flocks of embraces
in the garage, under the oil refineries
hospitable sirens, waltzing on broken silver.

And night deepened around the temple,
a yellow-black wafer, crust for the swans;
and the wind circled the olives, a morning watch
all night by the Kedron, all day by Euphrates.

And we'll meet again by the wintry river
where we swaddled the sun in a double wreath,
cedar and lilac, tangled in a knot of beaten
gold – sea-roses, breathing in Jerusalem.

*

Vines tremble in the night
around the house's wooden doors,
rustling in the soft breeze, whispering.

Otherwise, not a sound. The high
moon stands over the hurrying clouds,

motionless in the central dark;

the wind tries everywhere for a resting
place, vainly turning over leaves;

and someone stands there in the shadows
looking out at the dry garden, listening
to vine-limbs creak in the night air.

*

The Roman guards
cast lots for your clothing,
the way time and fortune
throw bones for kings' crowns;
you left them the shreds
of the Lord's farewell gift,
awaiting the shroud and the
spices of paralyzed women.

Your voice remains hidden
beneath the black mirrors,
diffracted, diffused by the
cold bones, the cold bones.

*

Between the parchment of an ending testament
and tongue-tied shadows crowded in a dream –
between blind feelers urgent in the city
and useless talent lodged in bitter syllables –

hanging, balanced on a grim little hill
among thieves and huddled followers, the Word
consents to dying in an empty theater –
to match the futile world with an empty tomb.

*

In a rough-hewn four-poster
the moody Puritan sleeps.
Down the steep dark stair,
slowly, a poor wife creeps.

Under a heavy kitchen box
there's a crust of dry bread;
strong hands undo the locks;
she goes out by the shed.

The old redhead dreams on,
kindly dawn slowly rises –
he sees a fatherly sun,
gleaming strawberry ices,

and a justified Rome –
while his wife, thinly wan,
espousing dear freedom,
succors an orphan swan.

*

infin che'l veltro verra

Aboard a swift Greyhound
adrift in America,
one of the grateful dead
plays a slow harmonica.

Sons honor your fathers
and heed their command –
it's a surplus contempt
that lays waste to the land.

Fathers honor your sons
and regard the heart's law –
for it's ease and corruption
that open Hell's maw.

And I'll sing the dark waters
and keep the long watch
til that Greyhound swings home
across old Devil's Notch.

*

in RI

No one will blame me
on the whispering shore
for lingering so long
near your small rose island.

Bees' slow honey
is the measure of summer;
morning and sundown,
by that rose double-arch.

And my tongue's dark island
leaves a late russet shadow –
dry relic of the voyage,
our lips' broken compass.

APRIL

Sunday afternoon in the gray rain.
I see a shriveled old woman,
hunched under a black umbrella
held tight like a turtle shell:

slowly she makes her way,
with each step her body lurching
sideways—and she's singing!
her clear voice dancing before her.

V

from
OCEAN STATE

CONTINENTAL SHELF

Mist and light rain
        over Providence again,
    outlines of maples
just budding, old houses
        blurring in the gray
    center whose everywhere
is nowhere else –
        sleepy neighborhood
    where I lie down,
listening, following
        drops down the pane,
    an easy curve ending
at the beginning, a lens
        for local motion,
    the urge of dark limbs.

On the California side,
        stubby trawlers negotiate
    shoreline under antique
stars. Sailors, between
        rocks and open sea,
    with kitchen, bedroom &/
or bars in mind, smell
        of salt fish, motor oil,
    muscling heave-ho
beside sun and moon –
        face it, everything
    you've got, net it
together, earth and sea

to answer your effort,
a steady buoyancy –

like the Point Reyes
        lighthouse, a tiny lamp
    the size of one hand,
inside a circular
        snake-skin of glass,
    1032 separate prisms,
each bending the rays
        to focus in a beam –
    120 watts in harmony
shining six miles
        out over the sea;
    from above, a whirling
bicycle wheel of light,
        24 straight spokes
    of silver and gold.

ORIENTATION

*This particular tree had pushed one of its ramifying roots
downward in a nearly straight course in the direction of
the precise spot where Roger Williams' head had rested in
quiet peace. There the root took a definitely circular turn...*
— Old Stone Bank History of Rhode Island

Everything dark in the fables
and shifting from face to face
like the walls of the earth
and the two elusive luminous
horizons. Gradually drawing
back shadows from beginning
to end the stories murmur
and catch together mingling.

When Eve gave apples to Adam
in the dream where only serpent
and God were wise and a harsh
sun beat down like a dull voice
on parched embraces leaving
clay to comb with heavy rakes —
no one remembers when it was.
Vines branch together and sway,
seeding the years with dizziness.

But like muttering and panting sweat
and the light of the earth's own
burning through bird and child
into the dark constellations.
Out of a murmuring planet a solid
apple-root in the shape of a man.

BALLAD OF THE DWARF ON THE DOCK

a rhumba

It's a small world,
said the little dwarf
as he stood on the wharf
and the flag unfurled.

And the sound of the surf
was lifted and hurled,
and the flung spray twirled,
and soaked the turf.

The world is a rock,
said the tiny guy,
and he glazed the sky
with his mental block.

And you may wonder why
he was taking stock
there on that lonely dock –
why should he even try?

The flag was flying high
like a silken scarf –
the President was Garf –
the people loved his pie.

But that heavy knock
of the waves had curled
and salt water purled
around his indoor clock.

And time was drawing nigh
on every dock and wharf
for every man and dwarf
to change – or say goodbye.

DOWNTOWN SESTINA

Downtown is gleaming, a nest of glass
Scant refuge for the homeless and the poor
Who trudge along under looming towers
Hungry, frazzled, begging small change
And subject to the better sort of people
Whose eyes reflect the glitter of the city

And so many circles animate the city
Captured in the high gloss of the glass
What's taken for the playground of the people
Erases every doorstep of the poor
In sprawling ellipses of loose change
Under the stolid mystery of these towers

Under the bright conundrum of these towers
These measuring rods allotting every city
Gyroscopes adjusting every change
By whirling speculation in the glass
The downward spirals of the ornery poor
Set stirring turbid shadows in the people

And shuttling promotions of the people
Forecast by divination in the towers
(Who's growing rich and who remaining poor)
Start dancing fevers in the chattering city
And snarl the artist in her broken glass
Frail craft undone by overmastering change

When fortune is the favored end of change
Suburbia the limbo of the people
And tender conscience faints before the glass
Rocketing skyward in pretentious towers
To serve the sleek imaginary city
Or swell the sullen rancor of the poor

Meanwhile the rhetoricians of the poor
In campus pockets rummaging for change
Inscribe the true authoritative city
And mint sterling mementos of the people
Studies wherein the mind serenely towers
Over safe specimens tacked up under glass

So let's raise a glass to the dizzy city –
A toast to towers, and all red-faced people!
And drink for a change among the homespun poor.

SLOW STREAM

Pull down thy vanity, I say pull down

You walk the freeway bridge
across honking Acheron,
thinking of Antoinette
Downing, angel from out of town,
dusting the tumbled structures
just in time to stave off demolition –

and there they stand, lifted in the palm,
beautiful hand-built buildings,
stilted memory, vivid yet
with carved and colorful invention.

Or you –
among billows of winches,
jackhammers – watch them tear the
concrete off the bridge
and lift the river into view again.

That slow stream will remake these rigid banks,
remind the builders once again – break the mold.

Follow the bronzegold leaves' free fall;
let go the framework – find your fluent home.

FOR EDWIN HONIG

on his birthday

A woman in labor
on Labor Day
gave birth to a poet –
what was she trying to say?

Lifting down that harp
from the Babylon willow –
how could we know?
Out of a babe's mouth –

Would it be yea
or nay?
Who knows –
maybe hurray!

Anyway, it was hard work –
she was glad he'd arrived.
Since then, he's conceived
a birth-song of his own – look –

it's there in the book!
The book of the world,
borne around on a word.
Happy birthday, Baby!

Happy birthday, World!

PHOENIX TREE

after hearing John Tagliabue read Walt Whitman,
Thanksgiving Day 1989, Lewiston, Maine

Off thin white leaves dusted with ashes
your voice tuned humbly to another's melody
like purl of spring water or
a breeze in the mountains lifts away
masks, poses, partial attitudes, goofs
of an artist at rest from labors –

and the harmonious muse of simple syntax,
the wavering lights bent to a planet's frame
stand free in your speaking,
branching, flourishing, essential –

a tree from the ash-leaves, eternal,
recurrent, here once more tendered from heaven.

11.27.89

OSIP MANDELSTAM

The priest, with melting intonation,
bridal sighs, deep shade
of bays, abandoned recesses –

the beardless one, the son
lifts high the censer, scans
the exacting responsorial.

And the difficult – the impossible
sweetness is born once more –
Harmony's arrow touches home –

O to be lifted forever
in the resonant ark,
your salt-stung aria!

TWO SONNETS

1

Faithfully he gave his life away
to life, and now those days return
unbidden, billowing at the stern,
forming a wide V of watery spray.

As acts in some unfathomable play
unravel in the dark, until we learn
to read the image on a burial urn,
breathing eternity into the clay,

his memories in a spreading pattern
lift a lunar corona over the sea,
a deep reflection no one can discern.

Yet we can feel the light of that day
blaze in the wake of an old man's glee –
a cup overflowing, come what may.

2

There is a city in the human heart,
emblazoned with bright freedom's heraldry;
her origin a midnight mystery,
descended from a star that shines apart.

As we have not yet compassed nature's art
of blossoming sweet flowers on a tree,
nor comprehend how life and death agree,
when, out of emptiness, one vital dart

arrows the daylight for all eyes to see —
so, walking peaceably together in the night,
gently we slip the traces of mortality;

slowly. beneath rose windows of charity,
stone walls of labor wedded with delight,
and the high holy days of human unity.

VI

from
MIDWEST ELEGIES

IN THE CLAY

Adam, under the rain.
Under the somber branches.
To soften, to cross out
the scrawl in the clay —
evening in summer,
buried, sleeping.

*

Your name is blind,
your name, nowhere.
Your name in the ice,
in amber, solid memory.
An outline under the
compass of my lips.

*

Blessed be the name
in the rainy dusk,
on the long road
under the bridges;
blessed silence
for hearing you.

*

Under the old rain,
motionless, lips
flower – a rose
in the slow night;
breathing, solitary,
heavy with time.

RADIAL

Seen once in the distance
behind closed eyelids –
an old country town,
afloat in the depths
of heavy black earth.

Speechless seeing,
the child's eye
obedient, peaceful,
nursing in the blood
such slow harmonies:

the rustling elms,
and houses ripening
in the summer light –
tentative longing
rising from the streams.

What equilibrium
shall we embrace?
And formulate what
loving circumference,
what fateful gift?

THE FRONT

When the front rolls in from the southwest,
spreading a wide fan of shadows and rain
over the prairie, the towns anchored
under the bulbs of the water tanks
and waiting for the downpour
to soak the fields, rinse
the machinery –
        maybe you'd be by the upstairs
window, looking out through the big black
bars of the oak tree toward the gash
of the river, moving there, hidden
between the steep slopes, the skies
quickly lowering.
        And Dad will get up
and put down the paper
        (ROOSEVELT SPEAKS TONIGHT)
take off the hearing aid, and close
the south windows downstairs (near where
the piano music curls on the bench) –

and when the storm finally breaks
he'll watch for a while too, leaning
against the mantle, thinking
of Kanesville (swollen
creek, fragile apple trees) –
while the rain storms down in sheets
on the grass, a silver wall
between the river banks, and thunder
rattles the blue chinaware, and Grandma

lights the dinner candles,
and evening hustles out the day.

From the upstairs window
maybe you'd see the strange
incandescence, the last
light burning through
beneath the storm,
and your face like a
smaller star, leaning there
against the clear pane –

MIDWEST ELEGY

On infinite plains,
among seedy barns leaning
on edges of small groves of oaks
just off the quiet roads, there
everyone knows, serious life
is elsewhere. *War* simmers
on the east coast, *Dream*
shimmers on the west, the rites
were unbelievably successful –
we fell in love with Marilyn
and Jack before their time,
they gave their lives, articulate
in the labyrinth – a consummation.

The storm comes later,
up from the south out of
the shifting void of the sea,
when the words are lost
in a tumble of low tides,
the glittering mirage left
drying among the fishbones
on the shore. Out of thirst,
out of the dry salt and dust
of unforgiveness, the storm
gathers into itself –
listen: dark silver sound,
against a screen of long-
abandoned, broken summer doors.

And what was I doing there,
riding my father's car
over the dirt roads toward
sundown, dumbly tracing the
scent of your skin and hair
in empty loops around the careful
plots of the abyss, my fears,
the sad compass of mothers,
fathers – this useless, neverending
unemployment, this adolescence,
my slow heart beating, gathering
desire and fright to approach
your ramparts glittering on high. . .

An angel with flaming sword
turning every way stands guard.
I remember our walk down the
narrowing point into the swamp,
behind the derelict drive-in
movie lot – two young adults –
and finding the torn-up porno
magazine at the edge of the water.
I remember fifteen years before
the fat kid in the back seat,
under the ghostly drive-in screen,
and the distant lights of Minneapolis,
kneeling long ago in the graveyard grass.

MEMORIAL DAY

It is no longer in my power
to pass the torch to those who follow.
Long ago I fell away from the steel
fiber holding up the school gymnasium,
and years have obscured the clear
path I walked, a serious child,
by the dreamy lawns, the sheltering
oak trees of the suburbs. Shame
weighs on me, tugs at my pride:
my tongue grows awkward, inarticulate,
unable to confess in clever numbers
all the grotesqueries this antic mind
would indulge – my soul, snagged
in a filmy web, in the seamy afterlife
of manifest destiny, that central pomp
of high-riding families, magnified
on the national screen. An irony
hovered with dark wings over the slow
river of my growing, marking a sign
on the brow of the elder son.

                        Thus
we plant our feet on the boards,
and pretend a scene. But every word
tingles with guile; the simple form
of the body recites from memory
a better tale – more harsh, more
innocent, exemplary. To be born –
to be thrown off-center – the rest
is only lust, or circumcision –

and perhaps a morning breeze, echo
and reconciliation.

Enter Hamlet, reading.

*Pray God, your voice, like a piece
of uncurrent gold, be not cracked
within the ring.*

The envious ghost burns for his
possessions – rattling armor there
on the far side of the battlements,
in the outer dark. Gertrude?
Ophelia? I remember Memorial Day,
gathering families in the clear
green stillness of the huge park –
and my brothers scampering, acting up,
waving their tiny stars and stripes.
As in a grainy home movie, I can see
my meek father hovering over the grill;
Granddad motionless, his hearing aid
turned off; and Grandma and my mother,
laughing, bustling around, two bird voices
diving into the water, where a bronze
Hiawatha carries Minnehaha carefully
across the muttering stream. . .

5.30.86

THE GRANARY

for J.P.

There were huge comfortable rooms,
dusty with archaeological bric-a-brac,
brass rubbings of the Black Prince,
and a photograph of your tiny sister
smiling, holding a shard in a trench.

I loved the cozy smells of your house,
perfumed with antiquity and your mother's
potato cooking, her high throaty
European sparrow voice, calling *Johnny!*
Johnny! Dinner's on the table, boys!

Your father a kindly cultivated man,
modest, his speech dry and bright
like a cello – questioning us
at the table with witty attention –
a doctor who treated *Guillain-Barré* .

We were twelve-year-old friends
when I became your apprentice –
careless for numb noon,
caught up in steady response
to crafty forms and riddling shades.

You inhabited a cloudy solitude
like a meditative Leonardo, yet you
marshalled all the armies of Europe
in brilliant colors for us to survey,
clashing and surging across the floor.

And all history lay buried in the big
Egyptian attic, that family granary
of Time, steaming through the deep quiet
sustained chord of Minnesota summer,
the dense last hours of childhood.

All except for the room set aside
for your older brother, with the bright
football pennants and the trophies –
a father's eldest son, whom I never
met, who never came home from Vietnam.

ARROWHEAD

A
maze of lakes in northern Minnesota,
crisp air adrift on owl's wings
between the wide gray skies
and a long swath of muted pines,
waves lapping, lapping
against the riding prow
of the motorboat, my father
at the tiller, smiling, looking
out toward the shore, quiet,
his beard growing rough now
after a day or two in the woods –

I'm afraid of diving too deep
back into the skin of the past,
my callow bones, the large
boy head full of springing
phantasms, upstart to replace
a sense of imperfection
with voracious all-devouring
enveloping thought – fishline,
this daily bread of blind birdsong.
Before you, Iron Range long gone, I
will always be that unbound, reedy son.

MORRIS DANCE

Every morning my father followed
the dusty freeway rings – a welter
of iron circles, a maze of wheels
dodging beneath the vertical
shelter of the concrete law.

And he jousted with the cold
steel cables of the elevators;
he stood before the judges,
spearing a wet dollar each day
in the rockbound pool of possession.

Somewhere between the inventive silence
of the shop, and the hollow hunger
of the labyrinth, he traveled out
with a ball of legal twine, ready
for turbid blades in the gripping dream –

and at the end of December,
the two of us, the rusty brothers,
trailing those roads again
in your rattling clunker,
remembering the dance steps

of the breakdowns, the power,
the glory, forever and ever.
A mystery man goes on ahead of us,
on through the green light,
into the lake-blue sky –

(and there's a charitable shadow
in the norway spruce tonight, a star
already hidden in the thunderhead;
there's all the peaceful sleep
we never knew, winging over the highway.)

AN OLD QUESTION

The war knew many theaters,
McClellan vacillating at the Potomac,
comic-opera Burnside driving the farmboys
up the hill again and again
like clockwork into blood and grass,
serious Lee striking northward
only to meet the Minnesota Regiment
and touch the veritable turning-point. . .

And then there was Lincoln,
best actor of them all, plain-spoken
yet with heart and mind in tune
for the mastery of gruesome Mars;
waiting for the war on the field
to end at last, his duty done –
and then let destiny unfold its hand
with an off-stage crown, a funeral train.

These lights cast on the boards,
amateur actors traveling up from home –
were the lines learnt well enough,
the plowing properly done that spring?
And the coffin crossing the prairie,
the wafer sun among the lilacs,
the warbling voice – sacrifice enough,
and memory, for the conflagration?

SALT WIND

Maybe you've kept the photograph of me,
buried in a drawer somewhere
in your mother's house – down there
on Lovers' Lane, in Alabama,
where the wind comes up from the sea.

I'm wearing a white suit
and a yellow tie, and grinning
in the sunlight near that island
in the campus pond – smirking –
your goat-poet, half-boy, half-brute.

And you were the tender wheel
of my feckless flowering,
and what was never joined
together is soon broken apart –
island from island, a wolf-meal

for the blind musician now.
See how your long back arches
thirty winters, your skin searches
my basil-flower fortress. . . that
front rolled on – this one will too.

How the spring sun shines in the picture
for my arrival, little prince
coming to say goodby! Leaves dance
on the hollow trees, the dense
maze of my dodge hides all departure.

I can see you bend over a small casket,
down there where the summer salt
blows through the windows –
arch motionless over this cosmos –
and toss the torn picture in the basket.

GRAIN ELEVATOR

O what shall I hang on the chamber walls?

I

Your voice, buried in the cassette,
Emerges, grandmotherly, dry and bright,
Lifting, carving out the unbroken world
In accents born of childhood flint
And cheerful apprehension –
                              your version
Of an early America, for Christmas
And far-off children – muffled
Collage of distant forest, echo's
Timbre and the deep snow
Surrounding the railroad tracks
On your way to school.

Down from Granddad's long-
Gone dancing days, you found
His songs of the Kanesville hands
(Where the long road stretches,
Veering through Iowa,
Grandma's letters in bluebird ink,
The farm just down from Herbert Hoover's
Place – an address he aimed at
Working for the railroad in New York);

You spoke of summer bike rides down to Red Wing
And your first train trip, to Iowa City;
Of songs and dances your scoutleader taught,
And skating parties late into the evening

At Nokomis. You told of a winter journey
To Northampton – watching from the window,
Listening to train-men standing on the platform,
Dream-shapes of late-night stops in Syracuse.

At the end, you read a children's story,
Ringing a tiny bell as you turned each page –
Tale of a magic Polar Express,
Hurtling north to the city of Santa Claus. . .

*

I remember on the living room wall
A somber painting from the 30's –
An eerie crossroads in the wheatfields,
Black skies lowering, traveling
Over the bent telephone poles,
The yellow grain flattened by the wind.

And I'm tempted to lift for protection
The heavy shield of your letterhead,
Granddad – your upright, spindly, old
Man's line beneath a show of power:
Stolid red and black, splashed
Generously across the top third of the page

Barnett & Record Co., Engineers
Specializing in Large-Scale Construction
J.H. Ravlin, President

With a landscape in various shades of gray,
Vortex of farm, factory, and transport,
Your tall grain elevators, flanked
By the docks of Duluth and the railroad tracks.

I remember the black galoshes,
The old raincoat, the birchwood cane
You let me tap the sidewalk with
On our summer strolls along the rainy
Mississippi bluffs;
I remember your hearing aid. . .

(So long ago. Letters
Only gather to a head, an inky
Swirl of signs –)

A late light on the River Road,
Horizontal gold, filtering
Through basement windows to strike
The massive blue-green maps of the world
You installed for us over the ping-pong table. . .

Granddad, I need your hearing aid
For my blindness – I want to hike
Beyond this jumble, on those chunks of slate
Engraved with the company name we hopped along
To find you, hidden among tall flowers;
Or follow upstream the River Road again
To a time before grain elevators, railroads. . .

(Your photograph from engineering school,
Leaning back at the card table with the boys
Looking calm and collected, whittling. . .)

II

One frozen night in February,
While the wind snarled among snowdrifts,
Small animals huddled in hideouts,
Winter birds trembled in windbreaks,
And homeless Americans plodded, hustled
Shivering toward what shelter there was –

One night late, my head lolling,
Tired from toiling over old fragments,
Paper scraps scattered all around me,
A wraith of memory looming on my right,
Shades of despair sliding up on my left,
I leaned back, looked up, and seemed to see
That prairie picture – lowering sky,
Weird light hollow at the crossroads,
Hovering over stark fencepoles, stones,
The brown road, the hard-bent grain;
I heard the hushed sound of the wind,
Felt menacing darkness – a fearful threshold,
Gates of tornado–no mirrored image,
But a wide-open window afloat before me.
When suddenly – something – a shape rose up
Along the fenceline – and I recognized him:
Dressed for weather, in a rough raincoat
And burly boots, walking stick in hand,
And a wide beard sluicing down his chest –
Eyeing me eerily under an old felt hat.

How strange! This varnished vision, slowly
Realized – while I, stunned in a stall,
Trembled, transparent, figmentary. A fierce
Confusion soon would have overwhelmed me,
If he hadn't spoken sharply, shouting –

"Leave it for lost! It's gone for good!
Come on, come with me! Move, move
And walk – walk through the phony frame!"

The picture was pulsing, wild wind
Raging, grass whipped hard on the hillside,
And he stood at the crossroads, rocking
In the storm, smiling, urging me on.
Not knowing what next, I got up and walked –
Stumbled toward the rectangle, glinting,
Glimmering gray, dun and dark yellow–
My feet uncertain, off-center, as if
I peered at a porthole girt by a gale.
I lunged past a lectern, danced around a desk,
And all was tenebrous – all but that picture
Aglow with the twister and Grandpa's eye-gleam.
I walked – but as I went, the image shifted,
The old man in the rain slowly receded,
And darkness deepened as I went onward –
The picture now a point of faint light
Ahead of me, above me, and I was alone
In pitch-black void – no longer my room,
But some stillness, a waiting emptiness
That felt more ominous than even the storm
The crossroads watercolor had foretold.

How long I lay there, whether sleeping
Or awake, I can't say. A long time
I lay face up on the hard ground,
Staring into the dark, listening low.
Then the first phantom came circling –
For it loomed like a vision or dream,
Altering before my eyes, gathered glowing
Against the blankness bent around it.
First I saw a shape, a rectangle, rolling
Out of the heights – but not the painting;
It was obscure – I thought it was a cloud
Or turning tornado, circling counter-
Clockwise. But as it hovered overhead,
I made out a massive book, fabulous figures
Engraved in gold across the front. The vast
Form floated in the sky, then suddenly
Opened – sprung wide as though some force
Had knocked the binding loose – and lo!
I saw pages and pages, countless, covered
With the same script, fly out
And scatter, spinning in wide spirals –
Scraps, torn fragments filling the silence
With a sound like grasshoppers. Slowly
The scraps grew smaller, flimsier – flakes
Of snow or a shower of dust, an umbrella
Of tiny particles shifting downward under
The book's black binding slowly rotating
Overhead; I rose on my knees and looked
Across the littered landscape, and saw
Amidst the dust a reddish glow, revolving,
Clockwise this time, a beacon over the dunes.
And a horde of ant-like insects were hauling

Huge chunks of sandstone toward the light!
The lines of insects swarmed in a spiral,
A moving labyrinth of stone blocks;
They were raising a tower, hefting
The whirling red light upward toward
The hollow book still circling on high.
And then I flopped, exhausted and off-
Balance, to the ground, and gazed no more.

I awoke with the sound of a far-off train
Approaching in my ears. I rubbed my eyes;
Again strange visions floated before me,
Blurred and indistinct. I saw a large table
With boisterous men circled around it,
Bewigged, frock-coated, each of them
Flourishing a feathered quill pen, one
By one putting their names to a document –
Then shaking hands, embracing, playfully
Pounding one another on the back. Then
Five dazzling, elegant women entered,
Carrying food and dozens of bottles
Of wine – there was music, merry dancing
(And all the while the monotonous sound
Of the distant train approaching). But
Gradually the character of the crowd
Began to change – the women were gone,
The men older, wearier, their clothes
Dusty and worn – and the dancing ended;
They gathered around the table once again,
And I heard one of them begin to read,
His voice broken, muffled – ". . .we
Meet in the midst of a nation brought

To the verge. . . corruption dominates
Ballot-box, legislatures, Congress. . .
Touches even the ermine of the bench. . .
People. . . demoralized. . . newspapers
Largely subsidized. . . muzzled; public opinion
Silenced, labor impoverished, the land
Concentrating in the hands. . . fruits of toil
Of millions boldly stolen to build up
Colossal fortunes for a few. . . possessors
Of these. . . despise the Republic. . . tramps
And millionaires. . . " The speaker stood
In the center of the crowd, gesturing
With his hands – but as I listened
His somber words were slowly overwhelmed
By the roar of the train, which suddenly
Burst from behind their table and platform,
Scattering all, demolishing that vision
As though it were a stage-prop tumbling down.

From where I sat the huge train passed
Just below me; I followed it with my eyes,
Observing each car and its strange
Riders. The giant engine itself was
Manned by engineers dressed in stripes
Like a chain gang. Then came the first car,
Crowded it seemed with farmers, lean
And hungry-looking men, talking, arguing
Together in anxious groups in the aisles,
Wives and children sharing a meager meal
Silently on either side. Then I saw
The second car—much like the first, only
This time a city crowd, immigrant working

Women and men, arguing, debating each other
With the same anxious excitement. The third
Was boarded and barred like a livestock
Truck – but through the cracks I could
Barely make out people, bent
Over heavy wrist and ankle bands, chains
Dragging them down. And yet there was
An undertone, coming from that car
A mournful chanting, repetitive singing
That sounded out across the tracks.
Fast on the heels of this car came
A different sight – an elegant diner,
Complete with wide glass windows, waiters
Tiptoeing to and fro, large white
Tablecloths well-decked with food
And drink. Inside, leaning back
Their heftiness on tiny chairs, puffing
Cigars, boasting, gesticulating – there
I saw the plutocrats – Rockefeller,
Gould, James Hill the railroad king. . .
Dozens of them, filling the car
With clouds of blue cigar smoke. On
A central table larger than the rest
Sat a bulging sack of gold and banknotes;
The big men crowded around it, each
With a well-hid hand of gambling cards.
They joked and jostled one another,
Eyeing their cards and the little piles
Of money growing in front of them,
And each occasionally swept up a small
Handful, tossed it to a waiter, ordered
Him to deliver it to someone

Up in the next car – which was a richly
Decorated sleeper, each compartment occupied
By a pair of white-haired gentlemen;
On the outside of this car, emblazoned
In silver lettering, I read: The Senator.
After that one came a military wagon,
A long barracks with simple wooden
Benches filled on either side with silent
Troops, young men and veterans; and in
The aisles the officers, commanders,
Generals paced slowly back and forth,
Their hands behind their backs or
Gripping the tasselled hilts of swords.
Then finally the last car rattled by,
Grimmest of them all. It was
A boxcar closed up tight, yet coming
From inside I heard human voices–
Cries of men, women and children,
Prisoners sealed up inside the train.
I followed that last car with my eyes
As it passed by, and the whole train
Moved onward, its roar growing fainter;
Watched it roll toward the horizon, where
I could barely make out the shape
Of some gigantic edifice – it was like
A gray-green pyramid in the distance;
And the track, and the train on it
Headed straight toward it, slowly
Shrinking smaller and smaller. Over
The pyramid, turning and turning
On its axis like some phantom, artificial
Moon, I saw the empty covers of the book
I'd seen before, disintegrating in the sky.

And the vision didn't fade; the hulking
Pyramid and the circling book remained.
So I got to my feet and began to walk,
Heading toward it, shuffling along
With what feeble strength I could still
Command. And slowly as I drew nearer
I discovered the pyramid was not a single
Building, but an entire city of towers
That sloped upward toward the pinnacle
At the center – the top of a massive gray-
Green ziggurat of hewn stone, slotted with
Rows of narrow elongated windows glaring
Out over the gloom (for it was evening
By the time I reached the outskirts).
I followed the railroad tracks, climbed
A small bluff, and from there the whole
City lay spread before me, glowing from
Countless window-lights. How orderly
It all appeared – the buildings rising
Upward as though by design on either side
Of the central monolith, forming one
Great triangle; and stretching out before
The whole length of it, a pool – a lake
Of pitch-black water, roughly triangular
In shape as well – so that the whole
Ensemble formed an immense, glittering
Diamond. As I looked in the water, I
Thought I saw large gleaming shapes
Moving – like enormous sharks, or whales,
But from that distance I couldn't tell
If they were fish, or just reflections
Of the lighted towers on the surface. So

I moved down the slope of the bluff,
Down into the valley of the city, still
Following train tracks. And when I
Had gone about halfway across the valley
To the lake, I was able to make out
Features of the place more clearly. How
To describe the all-encompassing
Hypnotic nature of that city! The vast
Diamond seemed to focus all its forces,
So that the image moved and shimmered,
Not like some hectic everyday metropolis,
But a huge mandala rising in the air,
Its light and darkness shifting monotonous
Waves. I saw that all the smaller buildings
Were similar to the central ziggurat, spirals
With narrow gleaming windows; and then
I saw the crowds – herds of people, marching,
Proceeding slowly, as though asleep, upward
Along the walls of every building. They moved
In almost perfect unison, sometimes
Linking arms; and I saw that as they passed
The narrow windows, often they would reach
Out with small scraps of paper, a ticket
Or token of some kind, right into the lighted
Window – and in return, receive some sort
Of food – nuggets of cereal, perhaps, or maybe
It was some kind of candy! But then I
Saw something more terrible. As the buildings
Narrowed toward the top, there wasn't room
For everyone – but the people kept walking,
Walking – and I saw from every summit
A horrible rain of bodies falling

Down, silently, into the black lake!
It was this, along with the slow progress
Of the crowds along the spirals, that gave
The whole scene its mesmerizing shimmer.
Only a few tough hardy ones achieved
The pinnacles of the towers – and I saw
A network of cable cars and helicopters
Shuttling from peak to peak, lifting off
The victors of the climb, to take them
Up to the very summit. I kept on
Walking forward, though now my steps
Were slowed with dread and horror – perhaps
I too would join the climbing herd!
And saw that the peaks of the buildings
Were all connected by intricate wiry webs,
Thin signal lines glowing in many colors,
And that the lighted windows themselves
Were flashing rhythmically from building
To building, side to side, as though
Transmitting complicated codes. Then
I saw the axis of it all – an enormous figure
Of a man! Planted on the central ziggurat –
A neon puppet, or some kind of hologram –
A golden cowboy in a tall white hat, atop
A bucking white stallion – and in one hand
A tangled lariat, which the cowboy lifted up
And down, slowly, steadily, as though
Dispensing blessings on the heads
Of the ever-mounting crowds. His face
Was gentle and benign, serene in majesty,
And yet so human, so approachable – like
Someone's father, uncle, older brother;

To behold his great figure against the sky,
I too wanted to start the heroic climb –
Perhaps I too could join the golden circle,
Learn the secret of the divine horseman!
Quickly I went ahead until I had almost
Reached the edge of the black lake – I was
Searching the shoreline for a boat or
Boatman. . . when suddenly a rough hand grasped
My arm above the elbow. "Wait," said a voice –
"Don't go down there, son." I turned,
And it was he – Granddad, playing the hobo
Still, smiling, still gripping my arm.
Then he let go and stepped back two
Steps, and pointed at the looming panorama
Across the water. His face grew stern
And he said, "This is the city of Disaster, son,
And those who enter forfeit their souls. See
The forsaken moon-book nailed up there? Those
Tickets with which they buy their bread
Were chopped up from that very volume – their
Throats are stuffed with golden nuggets,
But they've lost the meaning of the words
It once contained – and that's their doom,
To watch the puppet raise his lariat
As though to snag it from the sky – the word
They've bought to fill their empty bellies."

He turned with a smile, and took
Me by the shoulder, saying, "Let's waste
No more words on this corrupt phantasm.
Come with me, son – we'll climb back
Up the bluff." We followed the railroad

Tracks again, along a gentle slope
Up to the height of land. Neither
Of us so much as glanced around again
Toward the dismal vision, but looked off
Westward where the sun was going down,
Lighting the undulating land with gold
And gleaming silver on the long straight
Tracks to the horizon. We stood there
Looking for a while, and then my elder
Guide spoke up again, this time with
A quiet voice, almost whispering –
Remembering, as on Memorial Day, to mourn
The ghosts abiding on the prairie, the farms,
Or shuttling across the city harbors –

"I remember the funeral train riding by,
The black crepe draping all the doorways,
The women and children and grown men
Standing still on the roads, at the windows. . .
I remember the faces of soldiers
After the storm had driven them ashore
In the hospitals, waiting for life or
Death. I remember faces of country women,
Bearing up dignified in the lonely
Fields, the little towns of pioneers;
And the steady ease of workers
Lifting up each day with a deep breath
Of work, hard-won freedom at heart.
And I remember all those borne down
By the rain – feel the moving power
Of them, the meek, the poor, moving
Under the hailstorm, waiting out the tornado,

Keeping silence in their hearts
While the flood of philistine greed
Sweeps through on rafts of guile, waves
Of blindnesss – that great storm passing
Wearing the face of death itself. So
Be it, son: in a word, I remember life –
Waiting, watching and waiting for the storm
Of death to pass on through and be gone."

Then I remember feeling terribly tired,
Worn out with visions and long wandering—and so
I lay down there in the grass, and fell asleep.

III

Your two clay whistle-birds
Are on the windowsill,
Ready for children's lips to share
Their flute-sounds with the real birds
At the feeder, on the other side of the glass;

You've always been the better maker,
Turning the years and years around
With muscular feet and fingers,
Clay speech rising from the wheel
To last this generation, and to serve
The next Thanksgiving – plates, bowls,
Pitchers waiting to ornament
Some simpler, lasting celebration,
Open house for the upright heirs
Of tender hills and anxious clay.

And where's that modest watercolor,
Lit with the cold and clear Minnesota light,
Of Granddad's granary downtown? Standing
Behind the rusted parallel of the tracks
And a row of poplars, crowded out
By warehouses and condominiums,
Its curving columns burgeoning now
Only with air and memory – and hidden
Wafers of petrified wheat, noon
Sunlight answering a lifetime's work
Just over the treeline and the crooked streets.

On a sultry day in late July
In 1961– when I was nine – we stopped
In a little pasture beside the road,
Under the shade of clustered oaks,
With a herd of cows nearby,
For a picnic and a rest on our way
To visit Grandma's farm, and cousins
In Iowa City. And after the sandwiches
And sleepy talk, while the grown-ups
Snoozed among rocks and baskets,
I wandered off a little way
And found a squared-off family graveyard,
The gray slate leaning in the uncut grass,
Deep summer whispering from unfamiliar soil.

Maybe it was your voice I heard,
So long ago there in the aching depths;
Your voice, challenging me to find
That earthy crossroads – whistling word –
And lay Grandfather's brooding ghost to rest.

A VOICE

A voice moves in a heart fallen asleep,
murmuring there like a thawing rivulet.
I heard your voice, fluent in the deep
sweetness of the land, compassionate;
flowing beneath our cold, intemperate
harshness, the icebound lake of our death.
Meekness, only; poverty in spirit;
and over the abandoned towns, a breath
of life. . . When you placed a simple wreath
of memory upon this common ground,
I heard a wholly other spring, beneath
these grasslands, waiting to be found –

a vernal undertaking. We might bear
from hibernation something we can share.

BLACK MIRROR

I have a dream...

Amid the confused rustling, creaking of summer nights,
The stars' unspoken audience –
Builders of kingdoms share out their blood-light
With cries, with a slow radiance.
As when a star, tearing, burning the ripened sky,
Plummets behind mid-May lilacs. . .
– Afoot by the shore, the sea's troubled reply:
Apples – golden; mirrors – black.

Your hand grips a golden orb, the serious apple;
Your voice, uttering sleepy cries,
Moves like droning August through the people –
But star crumbles. Man dies. . .
And the sea, unraveling your voice between two shadows,
Wears out the green glass,
And rubs in waves of salt across the light windows
This black sandpaper loss.

Buzzing of years, growls of unremembered kings,
Breakers heaving curt answers –
We are cast out among detritus of things.
Under the white moon's pincers,
A green star quivers in the cloudy dome,
The black sail's insignia;
Your voice in the mirror, piercing the dire foam –
One kingdom's echoing regalia.

I will walk as we walked twenty years ago in the rain
Arm in arm through the cinders,
Around those hopeful lakes again, and once again.

Friendship. Memory. Dry tinder.
Oh to seal finally the dismal eyelids of the age
With a perilous, windy spiral;
To take a child's first step across the clean page,
Eyes lit with incandescent coral!

Along a bright trail ringing the grass mountain,
Voices, feet striking sparks;
At the hillside's foot – celandine, plantain.
Some ghostly shoulder, framing an ark's
Limber keel – ebony plumbline over the scattering falls
Of cloudy speech; sparkling rain,
Curved limbs muscle and horn below the walls,
Until your trumpet levels the plain.

And the wind tears the grass, and the wavering shore
Herds the sand back and forth,
While reverence of glass and silver blows no more
Emblems over doorway, hearth. . .
Green pools of broken mirror suffer the long junkyard
Years, glinting along the path
Of your river-song – Memphis blues, Nile shard
Still afloat, on a matrix of wrath.

To remember – day of rest, word singing out of sleep,
Limbs rocking, a tender song.
Tall cradling hills of stone, rugged and steep,
Fossilize the hopeless wrong,
Inscribe in flint and tumbling falls your memory.
Monuments, marble chariots,
Swirling of broken veins, of unknown infantry –
Such things of time appropriate –

Like this unruly amulet raked from the ocean,
A whispered Sunday in the sand,
Where a wind-cut lilac spirals in slow motion,
And a cloud, like a heavy hand,
Surges with shady blessing toward the disputed slopes –
Shouldering aside the idols
And drawing taut the circular tent-ropes
Over the offered animals.

Young lambs leap from the stalls there, near the sea;
Old men and the dodging kids
Fortify the streets with Saturday glee,
While in the shade, trembling eyelids
Close in silence. On the graveyard hillside, blossoms
Of cherry and apple crowd the blue
Crown of your garden – this prism of Jerusalems,
These meadows pacing shepherds knew.

Under cover of a whisper
Under wings of snow
I draw forth the star
From the velvet cloak
I draw forth the star
Of your protection
Black Madonna, Black Madonna.

Where life has fallen
And ships gone under
And clouds of November
Take flight in haste
And clouds of November
Shadow your cloak
Black Madonna, Black Madonna.

Who thinks you are gone
Follows their shadow
Far from the sky road
Your green star glimmers
Far from the sky road
And circles the children
Black Madonna, Black Madonna.

RUSTY EXIT RAMP

How many spears, frozen in phalanxes,
how many iron hills circled the fathers'
hope – chained waters of enmity,
cars harnessed for a pathway through the sea –

when, with a jesting wave, philosophies
of unsettled pyramids the fluted palm
of your promise whispers toward autumn
beneath twin-risen towers, O City of Cities!

HIEROGLYPH

Papa was always working on the house,
his long shadow bent across the sill
like a letter in an unknown alphabet,
his hoe or hammer making their steady
marks across the vagabond afternoons,
the deep summer water we lived through
holding our breath, our lungs tight
with promises, danger, laughing gas.

And when we grew older, more serious
and dangerous, Papa was always working
late at the office. For all we knew
he was a drone of the dread Pharaoh,
one of the caretakers of the Sphinx,
late into the night composing riddles,
subtle passwords and husky undertones
which opened the secret granary doors.

And it was only later, as we watched
his dry wooden boat slip underground,
that we understood the clean framing
of intention, the straight crossbeams
of its execution, that house of his
a kind of sounding board for praise.
Working across the tightrope of the
roofline was his way of walking on air.

BREEZE

A city before sunrise
hovers in the cool air,
under the modest arch
of early blue sky –

a dry honeycomb,
a gray wasp's nest,
hung on the limb
of some buried river.

Soon these streets
will swarm with faces,
laws and lawlessness
and careless artifice;

but dawn is simple,
native to earth, sky;
a sea-salt breeze
at the bedroom window.

VII

BYZANTINE
SKETCHBOOK

TRIPTYCH FOR ELENA SHVARTS

I

Some words floated toward me.
Trailed over oceans,
an ice-locked sea.
Your words, that once

ran beneath your tongue
from canvas near your heart.
(Whiff of cigarettes. Rat dung.
Wrong from the start.)

Aloft, to waver in smoke
at hobo altitude –
an image (hard to make!)
of God. In a bad mood.

Image nonetheless,
with blemishes.
And if he can lose himself
up where it vanishes,

among red leaves,
over nerve-streams,
bent, like a sheaf
in a Joseph dream. . .

I puff the mirage
back in your direction,
translated – world-image;
coracle; orb of affection.

10.4.95

II

after O.M.

I see the lame-foot masquers gathering
on a winter's night in the ancient capital.
Heirs and heiresses of royalty.
Blood of kings–and Sheba's parasol.

I hear it – midnight – toneless rumbling.
Ears razored by the rustling of ice.
So let the heart dilate. When eyes go blind
there comes a scattering of Paradise.

Golden fleece, where are you, golden fleece?
Behind the mast at an inhuman pitch
sirens weave the locks of Berenice, while
cautious Fates unbind – slowly! – the bloody stitch.

We shall be gathered with them, murmuring.
Snow will burn; offbeat hearts
rehearse sun's night. . . while stuttering
Time – Osiris, Pharaoh. . . beat a slow. . . retreat.

5.29.96

III   (Sham Death of a Minor Shakespearean)

"I die for the glory of the light and
the majesty of Apollo!" – he cried
– drifting slowly, fastidiously,
to the floorboard bedside.

Head flat against the hard oak
neither he nor audience could tell
if it was by his own hand
or by another's, that he fell.

Only that the heavy thunder, the light ringing
washing through his skull was not applause,
but penetrating phantom fingers
of the black – sable – nurse of darkness.

JOSEPH BRODSKY

But each grave is the limit of the earth.

1

You died on a cold night in January.
It was Superbowl Sunday. A supine empire,
Preoccupied with bread and circuses,
Land Rovers, stratagems of muscle-
Bound heroes. Next day, fire
Swallows the famous opera house in Venice.
Not with a bang – with a light rustle
Of red silk, your heart passed the final
Exam, black-sailed, in the science of farewells.

Snow falls on the fleeting moiré of the sea;
It falls on horsemen passing by, on the halfbacks
Of the dolphins' curved smiles (in a mirror
Of alien tribes). Snow falls on night grass
In the trackless pine forest; it falls with the stars
Drifting down from unnumbered, shiftless heaven;
So it fell, and will fall, on those bronze eyelids.
A guarded glance, coiled in frozen hexagons;
Shy cedar voice, immured in pyramids.

Snow mixed with tears signals a hearth somewhere.
Not in the street, not in this Byzantine air
Of columns and cenotaphs – no. Just a home
By a river of marrying streams; a certain Rome
Where tongues descend – ascending voices mingle
In companionable flame. This friendly fire
Eats brotherly dusk, shakes fearful ether
Into evening wine. . . one hawk's cry
Screams–and melds into the Muse's profile.

2

Life's flimsy laundry, easily
Unraveled. Transparent butterfly net,
Wing of a moth, how slyly they
Trap the hunter, iced on an alpine sheet.

You fight the droning in your head
With all the cunning you can muster;
Turning its power against itself, you lead
A life Laertes would approve (bluster,

Business laboring for acclaim)
Only to drown the voice above the trees.
Relentless, impervious to shame,
It finds you out, brings you to your knees.

And like the heavy signet ring,
A chieftain's ring, that hidden in hand
Sealed Hamlet's heart (O molten, circling sting) –
The droning issues forth its stark command.

You listened, followed. A shuttling pencil
In a nighthawk's beak – a spear in your side;
And a huge sea-moth with crossbone stencil
Shattered your lamp. Died.

Summer ends, the droning subsides.
The ruthless tango of prose and poetry
Is dead. Cicada shells, butterfly hides. . .
Some leftover spider's ecstasy.

3

In the depths of the Soviet winter, in the ponderous cold
Of Siberia, a boy cups an abandoned moth in his hands,
Born – to die a few hours old –

Into a false firewood springtime. Its delicate wings
Are only an affront to the divine benevolence; he understands
Nothing; his hands, like an insect coffin, bear the stings

Of the nails themselves; like a dry cocoon, absently,
They drift to the shack wall, and the fingers fan,
In unison, a camouflaged figure in the pinewood pantry.

This tender sign. . . a tenderness snuffed out.
This heavy icon, then. . . true mimic of an action?
Or only the swollen, distorted wings of a parasite?

Or only the screech of broken chalk on slate?
Droning brittle wings, poets take their stations
At the edge of the cliff – their noise intuitive, innate. . .

The butterfly is gone. Its form was here, immaculate;
The hands tracing its flight, aimless, serpentine,
Mimic its undetermined motion – late, late –

Since that double-woven fountain, afloat with indirection,
Surging, sparkling, translucent, seeks its mate
In a signal heaven – a camouflage beyond dissection.

2.2.96

OLD TIME ELEGY

Lord, we will write and write.
Your August ripens.
A radio keeps the beat.

The writing is what happens,
while merged with the wheat
a single strand of hair stays hidden.

WATER MIRROR

*Hammersmith Farm, childhood home of the late
Jacqueline Kennedy Onassis, site of the reception for
her wedding to John F. Kennedy and his summer
White House, is for sale.*
    – Providence Journal-Bulletin *(July 4, 1995)*

1

They're selling off the old homestead,
the mansion's on the auction block;
the lawns where Jackie used to walk
burrowed by realtors instead.
Ten million bucks, it can be yours:
the gardens, chandeliers, heirlooms,
John-John and Caroline's bedrooms...
Camelot flickers in the mirrors.

2

From harbor frontage you can see
four seasons glimmer in the surf,
watch changeless flotsam crash, drift.
Washington seems far away.
There, a bigger sale is on:
the common good, at discount rate,
from state to corporate bureaucrat
(by way of Senator Middleman).

3

So why mold grief in pewtered rhyme
for simple change, a mansion's fall?
Irish rumrunners, after all –
death by water. A waste of time.
A Yeats might mourn old manners gone,

the shipwrecked dream of Camelot,
and scorn the Newport plutocrat
gnawing mahogany's snuffed grain...

4

She's in the grave, the early girl,
swan-woman (pillbox hat, pink coat) –
sun-glassed, mysterious, remote,
demure, still point of social whirl,
who tacked astern with hasty Greek
to homeward islands, east of West;
she's gone, the *akme* of the best,
a dolphin–gilded, guileless, sleek.

5

But like a man who finds his wife
locked in the arms of a stronger chest,
I'm stung with song's unease, unrest –
a uselessness, usurped by strife.
Trajectories of melting ice;
chaos of shards; an arctic herd
shrinks (absurd equation) toward
Time's backlit Death Row device

6

and no one knows who killed the King
or the two princes at his side –
the talent that is death to hide
cannot un-Gordian anything.
Times are evil. *Redeem the day* –
that day he sat at Hammersmith
and merged the Peace Corps with the myth:
a green American sunray.

7

Another Greek, Simonides
(or so writes Roman Cicero)
wove stories intricate and slow;
his tyrant patron was displeased.
"Lay off those Twins, you dunce"
he cried – "Castor, Pollux –
you're labored, prolix –
recite my noble deeds, for once!"

8

And tossing the poet only half–
"Let those Gemini pay the rest!" –
the prince expelled the fabulist.
Then, in a glancing lightning shaft,
two spooky boys were seen on high.
Destruction rained down on his head.
The bard survived, to name the dead –
baptizing each guest with a sigh.

9

Another house is up for sale.
Driftwood clutters down the shore.
No one listens anymore
to songs of Camelot or Grail.
But over the mortgaged property,
over White House, pillar, dome,
I see two ghostly brothers roam.
Let slow strands weave their filigree.

7.8.95

FOR THE ONES WHO DIG

> *Mr. Tiscione's body was buried in Guatemala.*
> *The Embassy's version of the circumstances of his*
> *death was based on a report prepared by the*
> *Guatemalan police, characterized by State*
> *Department officials as "well-trained and*
> *professional."* – NY Times

He was carrying shards in his hands,
alluvial deposit, amygdaloidal,
      and may have stumbled on fugitive
constituent, digging,
digging gala beds, chatter-
      marks. August 22.
No passage home. Erratic block.
You must be brave.
      He was
in the tub. Idiomorphic,
honeycomb weathered, blood
      cleavage fan drawn
from host rock. Mandrakes
gather. Demonstration. Ghost
      stratigraphy. *Your*
husband is already dead.
No flagstone, hard evidence.
      A machete?
Combination of antidepressants,
lithium, blue mud, gneiss. Logan
      stone in the saddle.
There are
avocadoes
      in Aguacatan.

6 ft 2, thick glasses, hair
graying, foliated
      limnic deposits,
quaquaversal. He was transporting
Mayan pots to museum
      in Guatemala City.
Prominent families, clay
left in their care. Shrinking
      earth, paraconformity,
ripple mark, recumbent
fold, raindrop impression,
      reaction rim.
May have stumbled upon
worm's eye map, unconformity
      window, wrench
fault till matrix marine
transgression.
      *These people
have really suffered. I'll
tell you more about it when I
      get home.*
Suspected threat somehow
connected with work. Superimposed
      drainage, swallow
pit, tectonic culmination,
terminal curvature.
      Todstein.
She tried to reassure...called
at the appointed hour. *So
      sorry, your husband* –
gone to government office.
Requested two maps.
      She didn't have

the four thousand dollars...
to bring him home.
   Blank
embassy. Shark
teeth.
   Sorry,
sorry. Slaggy,
slickenside, soil
   profile,
spillway, solution pipe,
sole-mark, shatter belt,
   selvedge.
Hornblende.
Pitch.
   Rose
diagrams show distribution
of flute cast directions.
   Pebble.
Mantle. Natural arch.
Life assemblage.
   Problematicum.
Posthumous pumice,
rock froth.
   Paper-
shale, plutonic
plexus, outwash fan,
passage beds,
parallel roads,
river terrace, quarry
   water.
Obsidian.
Oolith.

Ooze. Red
clay (on the seafloor).
Rottenstone (for polishing
        metal).

Peter Tiscione. Bernice.
Amanda. Constellated. *Pietra*
        serena. Pietra
dura.

HART CRANE

1

Above checkered flickering of late
coffeehouse generations, light pricks
tap out a dim, midnight tattoo.

Is it the underbelly of a whale,
unfurling a turbid Mardi Gras? Slow
motion horns dilate for one liquid eye.

Answered by silence. Orisons
babble, fitful reeds rehearse,
recount your rendezvous

with a perfidious bark, while calipers
compress the extant manuscripts
(flagrant gulf no hands could span).

It was a weatherbeaten, Southern face
below the embroidered wash and spume
whispered the one word –

"follow." Upward, through vertiginous
mirror gardens – dangling fluted
routes of a sunken – forsaken Babylon.

2

Spinning, restless, coaxial, cued
to firewater, pried from pueblo
gaol, a primeval kachina leaping
into the blaze – out of time.

Hidden underfoot, to be quarried
from the subway, the broken stone
wheel of a ruptured earth mother
revolves with disjointed orbit.

Weft of vertigo, carbonized. Exploded.
Pronounced from wincing salt, faltering,
slagged. . . flower names. Fertile
reproof. Slanting, bedecked at last.

Volcano, livid, fluent, enlists
the police. Magnified chevrons.
Pulques Finos. Skulls look up,
fed your tangled battering ram.

3

Ironclad northern city in your nightmare,
and the sound of the sea, too familiar,
eager to lock you in a wavy ooze,
forlorn foghorn. . . such was Death's only ruse.

Who waits by the pier to feel your taunts
will always wait now. You waited once
for shoulders tensely spare, the tide's advance;
reposeful strength was gateway – into trance.

The bridge you strung beneath your bones
still rises, harbored, iridescent, out
of your twenties and the century's, still
delicately rides the storm. And Ariel
holds his song. . . and now Atlantis groans! –
surfacing with your ascending steep descant.

BALLADE ROYALE

"The enemy is seething at the gates
and all our stratagems so sorely tried
have surely failed, and rebels – ingrates! –
spit at us, and slink away, deep-dyed
in treachery." So courtiers sighed
and muttered dreadful news, in sheer
despair. The king was full of foolish pride.
All eyes filled with dismay – each heart with fear.

"Let's go unto the king – it's not too late,
perhaps. . ." So down stone corridors they glide
sharing the doom-filled business of the state,
to find their king. . . lolling, side by side
with his luxurious and mocking bride.
His eyes feign drowsiness as they draw near.
He snores – or mumbles something crass and snide.
All eyes filled with dismay – each heart with fear.

The great king disentangled from his mate
and leaning on one elbow hoarsely cried –
"Bring me my harp, O cowards that I hate!"
The instrument appeared. His fingers plied,
and with his long arm's curve struck, chord
on chord, such harmonies! – so sweet, so clear,
his servants melted. . . floated on a cloud. . .
All eyes filled with dismay – each heart with fear.

"Miserable souls – your anguish I deride!
When I am gone to rest – upon my bier –
you'll curse your God I ever lived – or died!"
All eyes filled with dismay – each heart with fear.

150

BALLADE INDUSTRIEL

Now that the world is one great marketplace
and all its treasuries (from sand and tar
to elephant and diamond, outer space
to ocean floor, urbs to jungle) are
for sale – now Party is turned Commissar
and Russia, China, even Cuba climb
that pyramid (from serf to millionaire). . .
Now is the time, O now is the precious time.

Now that computers prowl at cheetah pace
combing the earth for Cheapest Laborer
and every digit in the human race
must scrabble for superfluous welfare
and bide no time, by coffeespoon or star,
no time to dawdle, fiddle with a rhyme. . .
(you've got to get those groceries in the car!)
Now is the time, O now is the precious time.

When hoary banks account your state of grace
and future hands are cloning in a jar
and skillful engineers can scan your face
and clever churls can turn you into char
while mafiosi split their *wanderjahr*
between Manhattan and some sunburnt clime
one mourning dove still murmurs from afar
Now is the time, O now is the precious time.

A lame albino gypsy cried: *I lost my dear
sweet darling's ring – I'm liable for this crime!
Lord, if there's justice in this world – draw near.*
Now is the time, O now is the precious time.

BALLADE PROVINCIAL

The view beyond my pale, nearsighted window
reaches to the new people's new wall.
But I (whose people came here long ago)
see everything out there – from the Grange Hall
on the hill, down to where those shacks sprawl
soggily along the edge of that so-called river.
The owners change. . . the melancholy not at all.
Flow on, careless stream. Flow on forever.

Phantom February spring is leaving now.
The wind blows rough, cold – buds fall
from confused forsythia, frail pussy willow
– tears some plastic siding off the new mall
they're putting up – see those trucks crawl,
hauling out field soil (once so tender)
from Reverend's hobby farm (his final call).
Flow on, careless stream. Flow on forever.

Jackson kids I never cared to know.
Tomfoolery, mischief in the stall –
that's their world. Little Jasmine now,
she could have gone somewhere. Treefall
broke her spine, and spirit too. Well,
the bully empires of this world will never
add her to their numberless vainglories. . . hell.
Flow on, careless stream. Flow on forever.

The wind plays with the pussy willows.
(*Tell me, shapely tree, why do you shiver?*
No wind disturbs my steady, whispered spell.)
Flow on, careless stream. Flow on forever.

CHANT ROYAL

Through primordial seas, across illustrious straits
with pregnant sails flush with a salt sea-wind
and prow all curiously carved to meet the Fates
I journeyed there – where golden conch-shells bend,
and mordant gemstones shimmer in the gloom
and perfume slants obscurely from that name:
Byzantium. Up serpentine decrepit streets
I walked. Every feature (chiselled by defeats)
echoed the contour of an edifice torn down –
that dome where a spectre dangles, under sheets.
And that shell of a man was wearing a golden crown.

I wandered myriad days, mysterious nights
across the stony constellated capital;
beneath a full moon heavy with delights
I found the wise philosophers of Istanbul
each with many disciples at his feet.
The universe (they said) is incomplete.
It effloresces as our minds contract
which nothing that we do can counteract.
What's known is relative to that Unknown
consigning a King of Kings. . . to swing, intact.
And that shell of a man was wearing a golden crown.

Dizzy with knowledge then, I stumbled on.
Beneath the blistered placard of a Queen
I leaned against a wall, and the wall – caved in.
It was a tightly-woven shroud (I'd never seen
before, nor have I since, such subtlety).
A dark-eyed fortune-teller beckoned me
inside, and mocked my infantile intelligence;

her cards (fatal blows to common sense)
dealt me the royal hand (which was my own)
– upturning the Hanged Man (onerous pretense).
And that shell of a man was wearing a golden crown.

Now wholly lost, feet wandered where they would
on past imperial esplanades and palaces
down alleyways into the poorest neighborhood
where whitened maps and broken compasses
lay scattered through immeasurable garbage heaps.
There a translucent, anonymous rabbi sleeps.
Almost invisible, a shadow form.
He sleeps (eternally turning in his dream).
I enter there. In costume – as a clown.
He frowns. . . as though enduring a minor storm.
And that shell of a man was wearing a golden crown.

Daylight filtered through my misted glasses.
I must have dreamed that journey to the East.
Byzantium – straits of Marmara – passes
across my mind–fragments of a world (deceased) –
sails billowing with hot air – empty words
herded into buoyant phrases – for the birds!
Sentences disperse into their imagery –
imagery contracts into – imaginary
roots – boulders, pillars, parrots, columns. Broken.
Words. Mechanical. Bird. Rich Emperor. Menagery.
And that shell of a man was wearing a golden crown.

Morning lifted from the ground –inverted A
sent fanning through modular arrays
of crimson, mauve, gray. Over the old town
the sun emerged (orbicular) into a turqoise sky.
And that shell of a man was wearing a golden crown.

ON AN UNTITLED PRINT

for Sylvia Petrie

The work is finished in the dark.
The world's invisible, unknown.
A night of snowfall leaves its mark.
It will remain, when we are gone.

Inside the silver picture frame
frozen winter night has come.
An image like a negative.
Black ink feathered off, by hand,
imprints a landscape (winter gloom).
The traces of your handiwork
are what gives light – the glowing land
flows down (from hills to scattered sand)
in random touches. . . flick and fleck.
The work is finished in the dark.

This labor scatters into day
like Monday mornings – who can say
what these wayward shapes contrive?
Triangular, amid uncertainties,
one tiny house (snowbound, lonely)
gleams (nestled, shrunken)
between the looming cedar trees
and those unclear interstices
which could be universe – or none.
The world's invisible, unknown.

The picture hangs against a wall
where afternoon light sometimes falls,

and sometimes (strangely) time will give
instead of take. . . and I can see
what you were doing, after all.
Through curving space, look
back. . . into reclusive memory.
This house, this hill, this endless sea
were yours. Engravèd. Cold and stark.
A night of snowfall leaves its mark.

We grow away from home forever.
Epitaphs for each survivor
elevate the long perspective.
Parallels we harvested
return. As in a childhood fever
everything we once disowned
(what seemed frivolous, detested
chaos) now coheres. Nested
on a hillside, sloping down. . .
it will remain, when we are gone.

ONE EVENING (EARLY SPRING)

1

Late afternoon. I walk down Morris Avenue.
A blustery March wind hurries the clouds along
below a slate-blue sky. The dome comes into view.
It sits atop a sturdy synagogue, six sides strong.
Just then (suddenly) the sun breaks through –
the dome's half-sphere glows–warm ruby-golden
radiant expanding bubble – vital, alien.
Floats there, whispering – *I will overturn you.*

2

What if a comet tore through the atmosphere
today – smashed into Earth – a heavy sledgehammer
with one blow blotting out all, all we have here –
life, the human race, everything – gone forever?
This poem among the first to go into nothingness,
along with all other poems, all songs, all works of art,
everything built – bridges, those silos on red alert,
all cities, houses, races, histories – all drop to dust –

3

and suddenly national destinies come to an end,
and rivalries between peoples, states, companies, authors,
and the agony of becoming great, powerful, rich, grand,
and the monotonous jockeying to get the better of others,
and all the wayward labyrinths of love and desire,
all broken hearts, all longings and disappointments,
all the ideals of the whole earth, all hopes and sentiments,
all dramas, cries for justice – all this. No more.

4

But ghosts will remain. A ghost still walks.
A faint, unseen, unrecognized spirit
flits by ruins (a pile of radioactive rocks)
of the synagogue. . . *and enters it.*
Now the unseen has become – invisible.
Shadow, the shadow of a shadowy reflection.
Walk through yourself, I hear a voice beckon.
A seashore voice (papyrus) sighs. Waves nibble.

5

By the seashore, where the immense waves
address their manuscripts to the infinite sand
and roll, and scroll, thundering over the hives
of monastic hermit crabs fiddling the undetermined
panoply of Aphrodite (genetrix of these curving
clusters of honeyed birth, droning into mindless
cosmic sleep beneath an anonymous caress). . . and
far off, into air, dolphins – shuddering, dance – arcing. . .

6

I have walked, sighing, through myself. To the end.
Through the earth, to the end of the earth,
to the end of myself, to the end of the end.
The lost world, broken vows. . . all become earth,
at the end. The heavy stone flung from the sky
cracks against a larger stone (both broken).
You see the interstices (increasing, creasing again,
dividing, dividing again). One stone. A dying galaxy.

7

Around the synagogue in the evening light
the houses cluster in their modest drab integrity.
Walking through their vocations (under blight
of a voracious contracting whirlpool city)
the humble continue. . . gathering on holiday
outside the bronze double doors of their temples.
The writer (an unnoticed bystander) crumples
a scrap of crosshatched paper and throws it away.

And the wind lifts a corner of the scribbled page,
not yet finished with the end of the universe.
Over the brilliant dome a small cloud of rage
disguises the sun – cries: *I will immerse
in tears – I will burn with fire – I will erase. . .*
(– pretending once more deep within heaven
not only to destroy all creation and then
again rebuild the whole cracked edifice

but to do all this in the manner of a scribe
with one hand at his aching brow and one eye
peering at a mossbound, moldy parchment –)
and *Lord, we have deserved your diatribe.*
The parched earth groans for a comet's finality.
Your mortified heart stretches through space and
swelling spreads (ubiquitous) the fiery ointment
of your love, of your forgiveness, of your peace.

3.26.97

VIII

from
DOVE STREET

BRANCH, ALMOND

It begins like this, on a dark autumn day.
The wind is blowing, you don't know
where it leads. Pussy-willow, dogwood
wave their last leaves. The lead-gray sky

shrouds the universe in its camouflage
of sleep and melancholy. Ravens
mark your place in the book of dying
and being born. Goldfinch paces his cage.

*

In Bruegel's panorama, the herdsmen
follow a ridge in the foreground, drawing on
their oxen, charcoal outlines seemingly stolen
from the Lascaux caves. In the distance

storms lash a somber, mountainous coast
helmeted with desolate castle;
shipwrecks ornament the entrance
to the harbor. A wintry violence

looms in murk above muted ruddiness,
ramshackle roofs of valley and village;
Bruegel grins in the teeth of all this rage,
shepherding home his cataclysmic canvas.

*

Every leaf bears an image of the tree
(as when the underside of an autumn olive
stands upright, tall – a tiny silver cypress).
Every book bears an image of the Book *To Be*

and every child bears an image of the singer
(almond-eyed) who left a humming shadow
in the neighborhood – that summer cicada
shrunk to autumn cricket (fading, lingering).

*

Cosmologists are gathering in conference rooms
with maps and diagrams and arguments;
Anthropic Principle, String Theory, Branes,
Dark Energy vents, dents – various dawns, dooms.

I walk down Dove Street almost every day
to watch the silver-gray autumnal sky
mirror the shifting *moiré* of the bay
(soothing my heart this way).

Orpheus fingered the space between the strings
of his imaginary lyre (he'd thrown the real one
in the river, after Eurydice had gone).

Only a pearl-gray shadow (lightening).

*

What mutters and broods in an undertone,
the doves and pigeons underfoot, gray
wing upon gray stone. What flits off
at your lumbering step, O ponderous one –

through a gap in the trees in your heart,
under your eyelids, beyond memory,
beneath, behind. Dazed now, you see
but can't explain: *home again – Dove Street.*

*

As if childhood were Bruegel
panorama – tiny almond eye
planted (hidden) at the center.
And the passionate quest – trial's

puzzle of yearning loneliness
only subplot, type, analogy
(ink-path echo – shady
image – singular ingress).

*

Now the snow (pure, blinding).
Water *slown down*, retarded to
star. Yet I know you're there,
under the gleaming ring,

unseen. Where images fade out.
Puffy doves purr, *tut-tut*, bunched
on the ridge of a tree-branch.
Having you left. . . you're all I've got.

*

The war goes on, outside the brain.
Where the gray dove of Bran or
Bretagne once dove in.
The mirror's extra dungeon

for X, of X, in X:
stage envies, accomplices,
maybe lateral damages.
Machine read-out: *You're next.*

*

As if you were there beside me on the branch
I'll mumble and purr, puffed-up in the cold.
Because you're not here doesn't mean
you're not there. Unfold, again. Branch,

almond. Tomorrow's always,
and always is your birthday,
and this is all I have to say –
your birthday, always (little tree).

1.29.04

ALL CLEAR

1

A clear day toward autumn   after the thunderstorm
and forty years   after the last London alarm
a requiem   or a jingle   *when the peace bells ring*
and they sound the last All Clear   lips form

as on the mandrel of a lathe   the curving grin
of an iron horseshoe   and let the madrigal begin
again   around the reunion of a sounding shape
pounding across prairie   to a wedding without sin

and the seahorse full of seedlings   sends a plash
ashore in Providence today   a sailor's wish
it glides across the ocean   it's like being
on cushions   the vertical mast or   Yggdrasill

advent toward sundown   came after 40-ft combers
requiem for a blinking red-light century   somber
and fading   among seaward millennia   waves
goodby   hidden   like a wound from a splinter

of ash   on the central body   of an aboriginal Freeman
lighting the torch in a circle of seawater   a woman
swimmer   immersed   emerging   like a spark
at the prow   (meteorite or   bit of jasper-semen

red-eye   flung from green heaven   for the profile
of a horse at the prow   or forehead of Levi)
Eggertson's own Paterson   sunlit *Icelandigur*
glides across the blue   in a weird spiral

an arc   glissando   Arcturus   bears the whole
world beneath the mast toward the pole
star   where it began   sounding   flowering
on your lips   in the grasslands   so long ago

9.26.2000

2

Toward autumn   Vladimir's longboat follows
southward   to the Black Sea   swallows
return to the everlasting nest   and the word
ships home again   like a moth   toward All-Hallow's

Eve   a monarch   toward the cedars   southwest,
southwest   clay lips fashioned your nest
crooning over the crib   your motherland was
fractioned wheel of clay   spun first come last

from the Vinland barrel   tartar salt beneath
one motionless star   spun dry from tears   wraith
of seahorse Orpheus was   your seedling bridle
and   petrified pathway   a wooden wreath

of holly   one red burial for your eye   one hair
from the constellation   Bear or   Berenice
and where the longboat came to rest
Kiev   key vicinity   a port or bay   there

where the wind stops in the sails   billowed
was born   not *Sol Invictus*   but a yellowed
raven's beak   at the crossroad   (was
linen crossweave   swaddled in the hold)

where the mast stands   bent and listening
like a winded telephone pole on the brooding
plain   for the rustling of a whisper
(*corraggio*)   between wings   descending

for the child went forth always and   away
preserverant   down the path P (*Lex* Phoebe)
a spun-steel span for small harmonica   your
weird slip off the ironside   christened   *Victory*

3

Light wind   on the last unlucky day almost
not there   through crystalline backyard forest
chiaroscuro   time growing older toward
Halloween or winter   still   no breath of frost

but warm   Indian summer softest breeze
through frittery dry dogwood   pussy willow's
leaf-shells   flakes from dying ash-tree that
won't survive   another drought or freeze

and in the wind unspoken, children   a time gone
by   rustling unborn   a completely leafless one
back of my mind   circuitous vicinity
or neighborhood   (in Hopkins)   (Mendelssohn)

and my Itasca task   to recapitulate phylogeny
(tell us again   *ontology. . .   ontogeny. . .*)
schooled to the end this way   *a child went*
forth   (Phoebe, Alex)   into autumnal pageantry

Viking of pumpkin path   or lateen Jimmy-Jack
following the pebble trail   (perilous track
of fingerprints)   into the southern sea
so vast   (across his brain)   and tartar-black

as pitch (and so much heavier)   so that
the iron filings seeded on Cape Hatteras
would bloom in St. Paul (south of Capetown)
and a Planck-length plankton   sunken Ararat

unveil   its messenger: Armenian prow
a pristine meteorite   220 tons all 70 saw
(eyewitnesses) across the ice of Tagish Lake
free-floating in Orion ("slight return") right now

4

Christmas is coming   but here   in sleepy-febrile Florida
tied at the neck   under stage lights   one big brother
wrestles with another   and   *when this battle is over*
who will wear the crown?   as a gospel voice in the rotunda

croons in my ear   and as reporters cluster by the grave
of Robert Trout ("Iron Man of the Blitz") and you perceive,
ephebe, the idiom of this   intervention   (requiem
for a midnight sun   or century)   and through the nave

today   they bore a body to the columbarium
(rotund profundity beneath nine bells)   only him
(*Brown, William Wallace, Jr.*)   a homeless man
and blind   who stopped the wheels of the imperium

one day   right on the street   asking the father of
George W.   *please pray for me*   and he paused there
(the President)   and said   *come along with me*
to St. John's   *we'll pray together*

the music of what happens   when   *no man is*
and *the bell tolls for thee*   like Janis Joplin's
high note   *who will wear the crown?*   your doom
Kosmos   a little world   curls into bronze

and sounds   from the 132 rms of a pallid prize
to the 132 acres of N. Main Cemetery (Providence)
where you'll find me (here now   there then) mourning
a vagabonded   end of century   where a dove strays

from San Francisco   down to Florida   an unknown
hobo Noman   left behind   his leaf gone brown
is your redemption   (sleepy time and railroad
nation)   W.W. is his name   crowned   here   and   gone

12.3.2000

SWEETLY, NOW

Walking home,
head full of gloom
(my own woes muddled
with those of the world) –

noticed (on the sidewalk)
cheerful letters in pink chalk
(rounded, girlish – cursive script,
broken off – author skipped?) –

PEACE
    LOVE
(signed, in a heart-shape) *CLIO*

the Muse of History : as if to say
I'm starting over – here, today.

TEMPLE EMANU-EL

Unlike the capitol's bold marble, rivaling Rome,
your simple curve (amid rooftop vernacular)
peeks from the hillside; through tender air
morning sunlight sketches in your dome.

A line is only a figure for perfection;
Immeasurability need call nowhere home;
yet light crowns your six-sided honeycomb
as if to meld the bleakest contradiction.

Labor dresses, lightly, weighty stone.
Liberty's the child of constant care.
This gold almond (hovering hive-sphere,
so modest) evens odds to unison.

The burden of the Law goes singing, here;
mankind, infinitude, through droning time
fused in heart's foundation, frame a rhyme:
scenting ascents (attunement) everywhere.

AN UNFINISHED TALE BY BORGES*

*O Domine, suavitas omnis dulcedinis posuisti in
libertate mea, ut sim, si voluero mei ipsius.* **
                                    – Nicolaus Cusanus

This tale depicts a young man named Borges,
terminally ill, slowly going blind, unable to
decide how to spend his last day. Should
he go outside before the sun goes down,
and lie in the sweet grass one more time,
and gaze up at clouds, passing slowly
across the face of the sky? Or should he
open the book he's been meaning to read
(the green volume, waiting so patiently
there by his bed)? He begins to read.
The tale depicts a young man named
Borges, lying on his deathbed, unable to
decide whether to go outside, or continue
reading. Finally, the young man sets
aside his book, unfinished. The light is
going dim, golden. Trees are murmuring.
Soft air moves the curtains by the open
hospital window, next to his bed. Borges'
eyes are tired; he can no longer see. . . so
he shifts himself, slowly, aching, from bed
to wheelchair, forces the wheels to turn,
and rolls (wobbling, slowly) toward the door

* In the Spring 1943 issue of the Buenos Aires literary quarterly Jovanista,
a letter, purportedly written by J.L. Borges, signed "Julio Ciego", referred
sarcastically to an unwritten (oral?) Borges parody, titled "An Unfinished
Tale by Borges," performed one evening at the popular Café Manana by
the poet Ricardo Cesped.

** O Lord, the sweetness of all sweetness, you have given me freedom
to belong to myself, if I will.

NICOLAS OF CUSA, SAILING HOME

Never suppose an inventing mind as source
Of this idea nor for that mind compose
A voluminous master folded in his fire.

He was on board ship, sailing from Byzantium
when the moment of illumination came, a flash
of light that staggered him (as happened to Paul
on the Damascus road): when he understood
there can be no ratio, no means of comparison,
no middle term, between the finite and the infinite.
Thus, since God is infinite, we have no means
of knowing Him (invisible, incommensurate); so,
as Paul says, *If any man thinks he knows anything,*
he has not yet known as he ought to know.
It follows then, for Nicholas (*De Docta Ignorantia*)
our proper study is, to understand our ignorance.

I think of him in Constantinople, looking up
into that limpid sphere, that massive cupola,
Hagia Sophia: gazing back at those gigantic eyes:
Christos Pantokrator, hovering there, magnificent
in lapis lazuli, translucent marble. He would
have known that, even then, all-conquering armies
of the Pasha were encroaching on the city gates;
had swept away, already, the last flimsy shreds
of once-almighty Christian Rome – history itself
grown incompatible with that triumphant
image glaring down.
                    I cannot know You
as You are. But when I think of you
I think of Bruegel panoramas: there's Mankind
(a little, furry, muddy, peasant thing – yet
at home upon the earth – its caretaker – self-
conscious, quick – inventive builder, gardener –

blind governor – your tarnished mirror);
and, as he painted in *The Road to Calvary*,
you hide amongst us, suffering servant, near
the center of our troubles: buried in the crowd:
one of the roughs (disguised, in camouflage,
unknown).

HEIDI, PRACTICING ACROSS THE STREET

Spring plays slow scales, waltzes toward July.
The leaves obscure the branches, and the shade
obscures the leaves. Time's intricate façade
a busy undergrowth that blurs the eye.

Footnotes and erasures cannot clear away
her dense disguise, your camouflage.
Only a few piano chords, a forlorn page. . .
we're magnifying figures in some *Book of J*.

ST. GUILLEM'S DREAM

The City under siege
the Sultan bearing down
two mighty armies rage
around the sacred town.

Our walls are under-manned
the hard-pressed Captain cries
without some helping hand
tonight the Empire dies. . .

O Lord, let it be me!
the sleeping hermit said
as (rousing fitfully) he
gripped his wooden bed.

THE MAGPIE ON THE GALLOWS

Bruegel willed his last work to his wife.
We look down a slope of leafing trees
toward a weatherbeaten gallows, where
a small black-white magpie has alighted.
A group of cheerful peasants goof and
tumble waltzing down the hill, merge
with the background (sketchy, indistinct).
Beyond the rickety gray wooden frame
a May-time vista opens wide (vast, mild,
serene) to mountains, sunlit castles, sky.

Everything returns at last to the wife,
the bride, the mother in the landscape.
Mendelssohn – a dream my mother had
(her miniature oils were its expression,
the world I recognize is their reflection).
Out of summers buried deep, the longing
streams: the tripod of the firmament
rests on a point of irrational blind
balance: the magpie rumors – wars,
scandals – skitter across an icy surface.

Bruegel's image seems to say, the world
outlives our quarrels with our dying;
our quarrels and our dying flit away
enfolded in a subtler nature (one
we cannot fathom yet, but witness
here – peering into the limpid curve,
the tender distances, the calm horizon).
Remnants of an ancient controversy
teeter on the hillside. . . but the magpie
(casual now, indifferent) soon vanishes.

WHEN THE ARK TOUCHED DOWN

In every town, in every land and tongue
the priests and teachers purify the faith,
instruct the folk, distinguish right from wrong,
observe the ancient rites, deflect God's wrath,
urge everyone along the well-loved path:
but there was no such pattern of tradition
when the Ark touched down under the stars of Babylon.

The sons of Noah often disagree
and quibble over points of subtlety:
Shem, Ham, and Japheth share a history
of tangled speech, disputed property,
and *death-by-Cain* in field or dusty alley:
but there was no such habit of destruction
when the Ark touched down under the stars of Babylon.

The Lord, the Pure, the Power, the Supreme,
the Imageless, the One, the Sacred Dream,
the Holiness Who cleanses to redeem,
Existent God, beyond our fleeting sham:
we shape your profile, still beseech you, Come!
For only a perfect maze managed perfection
when the Ark touched down under the stars of Babylon.

DOVE STREET

1

Close your eyes   and step into my summer garden
(empty, small, forlorn)   come into my cloister
built of whispers   among chunks of dove-grey stone
from *Guillem-le-Desert*   and listen, now

to the cicada-continuum   hidden in leafy shade   overhead
a droning one-one-one   of winged heartbeats   eyes
closed   the threads of sound proliferate and
lose themselves   and then   (returning)   come around again

and where the small courtyard   (behind your eyelids)
contains the world   a heavy heart spreads canvas sails,
takes flight   like a gray brush-stroke   toward Yellow Mountain
or   as a fiddlehead uncurls   in chilly mud   toward the sun

In the abandoned cloister   your gnomon leads the way
toward noon   thus   at the vanishing point of appearances
a warmth exudes   light flashes in a spring   wounded, unwound
there   and gathering the earth   and all its dusty paths

into a balance   graceful, just   barely   there
afloat   like gnats in the evening   over a wide river
the particulars of every dream   that ever was
were there   with you   empty-hearted Orpheus

waiting   for the light-fall   the wing-beat
bringing word   of your beloved
from the grave of winter   embedded
in the purling spring   a sign   (J-fragment

from a fiddlehead)   the only sign
shrouded in murmurs   of mourning dove
or some Shoshone June   ghost-dance
here   in the empty garden   (at the entrance)

2

From your node of dove-grey granite   nestled in the Hudson bluffs
above the hustling metropolis   my saint Guillem
where the convalescent painter   painting so patiently
slows time to sweetness   and lights into the depths   I thought

I saw   it might be   something like this:
three young ballerinas   in feathery pink and gold   peering
curious and tremulous   around the curtain   on tiptoe
with unconscious grace (Degas, the Guggenheim)

and the young crowd's eager faces   peering   curious
and tremulous   on tiptoe   with unconscious grace
into the frame: there   in the feminine mirror   an iteration
of a golden measure   or   benevolent universe

the play's the thing   for melancholy Dane or Orpheus
hooked by the furrowed shadow   of an empty heart;
time slows   and lost is action   to the name, unspeakable
and grey (like the shimmer of Law   in the dolphin-depths)

*all's figure*s   cries the street-wise idiot
when the heartbroken hero   descends into the grave:
for the one who went before   already lifts him free
in the slivered glint   of every new year's day

and O what mighty wooden O is this   resting on a Sabbath-ship
a ring-dance   ringed around a painted pose   a pause
or cloistered clustering   around a single coiled spring
a noon   where an ink-brush runs   a stream   upstream

to a sunny mountain: what gives   which gives   who gives
and gives   and flows *perpetuum mobile*   continuum's
heart's blood O   hearty *sacrificium*   full, complete and
with unconscious grace   (inflected law   of every lovely feat)

3

Omnia enim universalia, generalia atque specialia in te
Iuliano iulianizant [All universals, generalities, and specifics
julianize in you, Giuliano]   – Nicolaus Cusanus

A faint gray pencil-sketch   my mother made   decades ago
floats in a blue corner: two redhead brothers   like twins
almost an octave   Guillem & Giacomo   sit   parallel
each sketching (right-handed)   intent   upon   blank white

& Gong Xian   abandoned the field   and the fugue of war
(a change of ancient dynasties   Ming for Shang)
trailing retreat   transmuting each desire
(only flickers   of black horsehair)

the Yellow Mountain was   left to your imagination
in grey-black flecks   and war and peace   the blank
spaces   the crooked lightning paths   left up to you
(your willing hand   your loving heart   your sight)

Leonardo drew (lefty, *mancino*) the faintest of red lines
beneath the leaning eyes of Mary   bending down
(seraphic)   toward the babe: his notes
a kind of mirror-writing (*all'ebraico*)   with "tired hand"

And in the wintry womb   the gray-black limbs
iterate (tired, crooked) against the snow   a backward trail
or trial   a coiled, cold metal spring or   trapper's guile
(elusive prey   grey shadow   fleeting   glimmering)

low cooing   from a frozen eave or   looking-glass
intones an octave   twinned in unison   (some mournful-
silver marriage rite):   a thread of golden lightning
through an ocarina   to a painted ear (and scandalized)

announces stormy weather   thunderstorms and   thaw
across the mountains   where waterfalls   rush
past banks of cedars, reeds   (your brush with
fate   by horsehair   led you   here)

                    4

A washed-out February light   winter floating away slowly
and the sound of a mourning dove   *one   one-one*
mingled with elisions of an iron brake   *life's nonsense*
and my notes   cars on the road

a world gone quiet   in my mind   (preparation
for annunciation)   spring's in the womb
of sister-dove: limping slowly on the barren earth
she goes   as if she had a stone in her shoe

maybe   a stone fallen from heaven
landed in a camel-canopy   Abram's *otfe*
out of Ur for good   across the sandy waste
under the fringed silk   she sits in shadow

cooing to the warriors   urging them on   to the end
of their beginnings   all the way to Jordan
or Jerusalem   where they guard the black stone
of the scapegoat   (father, son and   intervening angel)

another stone   too heavy for heaven   and buried deep
in your corrupted heart, O   horseman, knight:
love is reason   and reason is love,   she coos
and this equality   brings Jubilee,   she whispers

where seven iron rings   circle the sacred city
each ring manacled to its own   unbreakability
(like weapons of mass destruction   guarding
weapons of mass destruction)   *from the days of John*

until now   the Kingdom has come with violence
violent men   take it by force   but it shall not be so
with you   murmurs the fragile   enshrouded bird
(grey wing   buried in grey stone   furled   in black)

5

i.m. Richard L. Champlin

He came to rest   (meek one)   in an abandoned orchard
alongside a stone wall   in Foster   in the dog-days
of August   his hand atop a sapling   a full box
of peaches at his side   the perfect naturalist

come (ripened) to his hour   out-of-doors
and maybe the orchard   harbored apple trees
like Blackstone's *Yellow Sweeting*: he would know
having discovered a red-flowered Spicebush

(*Lindera benzoin forma rubra R.L. Champlin*)
and the national champion Pussy Willow
maintained records of notable trees
exceptionally astute and persistent observer

birds, turtles, and butterflies   very good storyteller
diligent keeper of written records (daily journals
amounted to 35 vols.)   companion to most
of the old Yankees from northwestern Rhode Island

local lore and cultural history   locations of springs,
Native American mortar stones, threshing rocks,
charcoal mounds   reverent, modest, and private man
Redwood Library director   *botany, ornithology,*

mycology, entomology, malacology, ecology
so you might sketch a quick landscape
beneath Yellow Mountain   with the tiny figure
of the scholar   hidden there   contemplative

eye   beholding   mirrored   beheld now   in your eye
the absent shadow of your twin   *your spouse*
(Blackstone for Guillem   Eurydice for Orpheus)
(apples in a cloistered garden   *sister-dove*)

Note: lines in italics from obituary by Peter Lockwood,
published in *Rhode Island Naturalist*, v. 10 n. 2 (Nov. 2003).

IX

LATE NEWS

THE LIBRARY

On the downward slope of an August wave,
in the windblown backyard (a vacant lot
of frowzy ferns, pinched black-eyed susans)
I close my book. . . an image surfaces.

October twilight, far-off, deaf-mute.
Obsolete as ancient Alexandria.
Low booms of shunted steel, tumbling
(train depot, Minneapolis Moline). Flat
fields like rusty planetary rings – waiting,
subdued and saturnine, for snow. It's late –
after school, piano lesson. I'm walking
with my mother up the sidewalk, under high
oak trellis, rasping leaves. Maroon two-storied
brick, with spiral staircase, lookout cupola.
The library sits there, off by itself
along a ridge above the railroad yard.

Inside, chatter of racing, raucous children.
Cozy warmth of lamps above looming shelves.
The tall, sharp-eyed librarian, hovering like
a heron at the end of wooden aisles, wreathed
in the peat-bog scent of popular favorites.
I resolutely stomp upstairs, to the Older
Readers' Room, zeroing in on *Cowboy Bob*.

Only a shell, time's snail-pace carapace,
her modest midwestern façade, our civic
edifice. Inside, the expanding universe
of wide-eyed plains – palmetto groves – blue
tiers of Norway pine. . . thus plum-colored
bricks unpin the fan of Scheherazade.

And it seems my memory, our memories,
are stored up there, as autumn comes on.
Just as the ghostly palpitation of a Jack
o'lantern lures the last of the moths,
we are reeled inside, we are taken in.
Up to the too-familiar, foretold dénouement –
bedtime, little Bookworm – turn out the light!
Feet beyond the door *diminuendo* (autumn rain).

ATLANTIS

It was behind the slough, where we floated
the raft – where we swung the tire-swing
over clay-brown slime (that muddy pond).
A miniature upland meadow. Grass waves,
milkweed lighthouses... ragged frieze
of stray unbroken apple trees, let out to
graze. *Summer night, Atlantean* (remote,
somewhere). Heidi invited us. The girls
had orchestrated everything (flashlights,
nets, jars) – so we trailed along, into their
quaint galaxy. Coltish laughter, shimmer
of *Salomé*-grass. *Ukiyo*... paper-lantern
ambience. When we gathered fireflies
under firefly stars (garnet, violet, marine).

ARMY MEN

in memory, Edward S. Gould

His fisherman's hands, speckled with age spots
like a golden trout. A redhead once, he was
a man of autumn colors, steeped in yellows,
browns, reds. In his castle-apartment, hazy
with pipe fumes, light through old curtains
winked from his clock, his guns, his brass
shell case. One Christmas, he & Grandma
gave us each (Jimmy & me) a giant box
of *army men*. Jimmy got the Revolution;
I got World War One. I threw a tantrum –
wanted *Jimmy's* war! Mom rousted me
upstairs. I wailed & wailed... 'til Grandpa
ventured up. & so the veteran of St. Mihiel,
the Argonne drive, went *over there* once more.

BAGHDAD EPITAPH

I suppose you could call me a human shield:
I prevented a bullet from hitting a wall.
I got in the way searching for water.
It wasn't my game plan at all.

I got in the way of so many things:
empire, democracy, dictatorship
rivalry, vengeance, propaganda
(somebody's ego-trip).

I lie in a dusty Baghdad street.
Bosses drive over, wave after wave.
Here is the cradle of civilization.
Here is my early grave.

STARS IN THE EARTH

homage to Tomas Tranströmer

The quiet Swede goes for an evening walk.
It's growing dark already, cold.
Far off, a silent bivouac of trees, asleep
beneath snow-blankets. The gray sea, whimpering.

Overhead, tiny train-lights of stars
skim past the dark station, toward unmapped regions.
His feet slush through old shelves of ice. He feels
the planet sleepwalk – muttering, dreaming, sailing on.

On a gray-green brow, a lonely farm opens one eye.
A star has made its nest on earth. And now
more lights... a constellation swims into the forest.
He'll christen it "the Hearth" when he gets home.

FERMAT'S LAST POEM

I have written a truly marvelous poem
which this margin is too narrow to contain.

EVERYTHING, EVERYWHERE

Some Saturday evening, summer, years ago.
When you are small, everything seems larger.
Closer. Alive to the touch (as in a dream).
There was a painting in my parents' house.
A painting of a house. At dusk. Hidden,
lost at sea. In the anonymous ocean
of the farmland. As dark as it could be.
The palest of pale yellow light crept out
through a small window, into a mud-green
yard. A kitchen door. A pickup truck
under the cloud-crown of a brooding elm.
A voice calls through that window. When
you are a child, everything draws near. A
light wind through the dusk is everywhere.

ALFALFA

The picnic table in the stalky growth
between soft-needle pines, somewhere
west of Duluth. On our way north.
At the weatherbeaten drive-in (finally out
of the stifling station wagon). Somehow
the place lingers in mind. Maybe
the bareness, pine-scent, plain
planks of the diner latch onto later,
East Coast lobster traps… Cape Cod?
More likely, something happened there.

A wispy, fussy lad with a large forehead
(cowlick) looked off into a blue-green
grove, Italianate. Felt
the wind push on, flow by
through stiffening field grass.

JÓZEF CZAPSKI

Limpid Paris, long before the wars.
The capital drowses in a blooming haze.
Overcome by ailments and insomnia
(the madeleine still in his hand, the tea
still steaming on its tray) Marcel
nods off. Awake or dreaming? He can't tell.

Only a rest note of lost time.
Soft arcs of summer fountains seem
to darken into thunderclouds, or blood;
sealed retinas project a grimmer mood.
The prison camps, the death trains, fields
of terror... Sleep's apocalypse unfolds.

Marcel groans in his dream. Who's this?
Etched profile of a sketching artist.
Can it be Elstir, Balbec's grand old man?
Someone younger, scratching with a pen –
mild-mannered beanpole, thin as tamarack.
He aims to bring some Polish children back.

Who can it be? Noble Sigismundo?
Prince of Warsaw (*la vida es sueño*) –
whose manacled soul dreamt itself free
of tyrannical *padre*, jealous Muscovy?
No, no... some unknown soldier.
Diamond light glints in Marcel's mind-door.

He might have passed the young man in the street.
He might have met him in some suite
in St. Germain. A penniless aristocrat
from vast, remote, childhood estate
who fled to Paris, and began to paint...
read Proust. War came, and home he went

to fight for Poland. Captured by Soviets.
Flung into the camps. The more he forgets,
the more he remembers... a saving angel
of civilization guides him across hell.
He whispers so, to famished prisoners,
Coraggio – how memory restores...

Marcel's eyelashes flicker in the stream.
A line from Poe. *A dream within a dream.*

AUTUMN

The crickets were ringing their tiny glockenspiels
through the parish dusk. Summer was stroking
a late self-portrait in the Seine's smaragdine
bends. The gloomy waiting mothership
traced the twin outlines of her absent coronet.

Autumn was on its way. And we wondered when
some *douce enfant* might pirouette again
across the umbilical rainbow of her labyrinth.

ABOUT THE AUTHOR

HENRY GOULD, a Minneapolis native, returned to Minnesota in 2015 after 45 years in Rhode Island. His poetry, essays and reviews have appeared in journals such as *DiVersos, Poetry, Rain Taxi, Jacket, Notre Dame Review, West Branch, Boston Review, Mudlark,* and *Critical Flame.* Three books have been published : *Stone* (Copper Beech Press, 1979), *Stubborn Grew* (Spuyten Duyvil, 2000), and *Ravenna Diagram I-III* (Dos Madres, 2018-2020). For 10 years he co-edited (with Janet Sullivan) the Rhode Island literary magazine *Nedge.* He also edited and published the collected poems of poet and translator Edwin Honig (*Time & Again : Poems 1940-1997*).

OTHER BOOKS BY HENRY GOULD
PUBLISHED BY DOS MADRES PRESS

Ravenna Diagram -volume I (2018)
Ravenna Diagram - volume II (2018)
Ravenna Diagram - volume III (2020)

FOR THE FULL DOS MADRES PRESS CATALOG:
www.dosmadres.com